Dedicated to Leda and Luigi Giannasi, Marco's parents
Pictured, Canasta 1956

Dining Tales

Marco Giannasi   Alex Meikle

Copyright © 2024

All rights reserved.

ISBN: 9798328113465

All rights reserved, including the right to reproduce this book, or any portion thereof in any form. No part of this book may be reproduced, transmitted, downloaded, reverse engineered, or stored, in any form or introduced into any information storage and retrieval system, in any form or by any means, whither electronic or mechanical without the express written permission of the authors.

PREFACE

GORDON MACINTYRE

Gordon McIntyre is the founder of Hospitality Health, a charity supporting staff within the hospitality industry. Prior to this, he was 30 years in Further Education at City of Glasgow College (formerly Glasgow College of Food Technology), a college that has trained hundreds of young people in preparation for the challenges of the sector.

What an amazing collection of stories Marco and Alex have gathered in Dining Tales. It highlights the great and good of Glasgow's hospitality and restaurant scene. Each one of them is a name that will be well known to all in Glasgow and beyond, even if you are not a "foodie". It is amazing the number of extremely successful restaurant operators and chefs Glasgow has produced over the years…..and is still producing.

They have all worked extremely hard at their business and listened to their guests along the way, ensuring they are offering the right menu choices, ambience, and service to the customers. They have developed the offer as they progressed through the years, always adapting to what was required, ensuring the business continued to be successful. For many the hours were long, kitchens small and uncomfortable, restaurants tightly cramming an extra table in when it was possible. A tough career path to be following. It took passion, grit, determination, dedication, energy, and empathy to succeed both then and now.

Things are however changing, 2020 saw businesses closing and guests being told to stay at home as COVID hit the UK and everything changed. As many of the chefs and restauranters reflect in the following pages, life in catering could be tough and harsh. As we move forward post covid things have got to be different. Staff and teams require to be managed in a different way. Empathy is now so important in the business of hospitality; wellbeing has become a new term that has emerged where owners and managers are supporting the wellness of employees in more compassionate ways. And as is borne out by their testimonies in *Dining Tales* this new approach significantly boosts morale, encourages good teamwork, is far better for recruitment and improves quality and service for customers. Everyone wins.

On a personal note, I have known Marco Giannasi for quite some time and hugely admire the journey he and his family have been on. *L'ariosto* in the city centre, one of the restaurants he has managed, was a legendary venue in Glasgow, providing the traditional Italian offer the city enjoys so much. My personal highlights included the steak Diane, and Crepe suzette from the flambe.

Dining Tales is arriving on the scene at a perfect time, one to allow reflection on the past as we move towards a new chapter in the restaurant and hospitality scene. It is full of wonderful stories, highlighting stressful and worrying times, educational advice, and funny anecdotes. A perfect book for your coffee table, for you and any visitors to your home to read.

ABOUT THE AUTHORS

Marco Giannasi is the successful proprietor of the Battlefield Rest restaurant. Marco transformed a dilapidated former tram halt into a very popular Italian eatery which has become a landmark for diners both in the south-side and further afield.

He has also conserved an iconic building in the Battlefield area and, indeed, has made part of it an apiary which produces locally produced honey and helps preserve the local bee population.

He has recently turned his hand to writing short stories with a distinctive culinary theme.

Alex Meikle was formerly a CEO of several third sector social care organisations in Glasgow. He also spent many years working in the addiction services in the city and has just recently retired. He still provides a consultancy on social care and community-based issues.

Alex's main interest is writing, and he published his first novel, Deception Road, which is a political thriller set in Glasgow, in 2017. This is the first of four thrillers centred on the career of MI5 officer, Eddie Macintyre. The second novel in the quartet, Caledonia Smack, will be released soon.

Acknowledgements

The authors would like to thank all the contributors for giving us their time and supplying such fascinating and engaging stories about their industry.

We would also like to thank the following whose help has been invaluable:

Andrew Hamilton, the Director and Senior Designer of 13 Thirteen Design for cover design and graphics and website support.

Frank Chambers for taking our raw Word files and photos and turning them into a book.

Brian Welsh the "Helensburgh Wanderer" for assistance with press releases and media support.

Marisa Giannasi, Creative Director of Method Studio, for the cover art work.

MANY THANKS TO OUR SPONSORS

Alison Chisholm, Reaside Chisholm Solicitors

Mario Telese, Coffee Solution

Vari McGale, Loop Recycling

Ross MacLeod, MacLeod Lettings

Paul Hodgkiss, Paul Hodgkiss Designs

Luigi Carnevale, Carnevale Ltd

Walter Pessina, Continental Wine (CWF) Ltd

Micheal Migo, Migo Sports

Stephen Usher, KPP Accountants

Warren Paul, Paramount Design and Print

Paul Fitzpatrick, Hine Cognac

Stuart Cassidy, Spartan Protein

Glasgow Taxi Operators Association

Contents

INTRODUCTION: 1

1. JOHN QUIGLEY: NO TEARS WITH THIS RED ONION 5

2. GIOVANNA EUSEBI, EUSEBI'S DELI: EAST & WEST, FRESH IS THE BEST 11

3. SARTI: A GLASGOW ITALIAN JOURNEY 17

4. THE STORY OF THE COIA'S: FOUR GENERATIONS OF A DINING LEGEND 27

5. DOMENICO CROLLA: A LICENCE TO SERVE PIZZA 35

6. MICHELE PAGLIOCCA: NEVER A DULL MOMENT IN THE TEAROOMS 45

7. GRAEME CHEEVERS & UNALOME: THE PATH TO FINE DINING IN GLASGOW 56

8. RYAN JAMES AND THE BUTTERY: REVITALISING A GEM IN THE CITY 63

9. SEUMAS MACINNES AND CAFÉ GANDOLFI: A JEWEL AT THE HEART OF THE MERCHANT CITY 72

10. PAUL STEVENSON: PAESANO PIZZA, THE MAN TAKING PIZZA TO NEW LEVELS 79

11. GILLIAN EAGLESON: SCOTLAND'S FIRST FEMALE EXECUTIVE HEAD CHEF IN A FIVE-STAR HOTEL 85

12. MARCO GIANNASI: REST & BE THANKFUL ON THE SOUTH SIDE OF GLASGOW, THE BATTLEFIELD REST 94

13. JEN DOHERTY & ALEX MATHESON: IN WITH THE NEW AT THE BATTLEFIELD REST ... 103

14. GUY COWAN: KEEPING IT SIMPLE ... 113

15. NATALINO CELINO: FOUNDING A GLASGOW LEGEND ... 126

16. CHRIS MARTINOLLI, SHINING A LIGHT THE ITALIAN WAY: THE MAN BEHIND LA LANTERNA ... 132

17. PETER MCKENNA AND THE GANNET: HIGH END IN THE WEST END ... 141

18. ZOLTAN SZABO: THE MASTER CRAFTSMAN OF FOOD ... 150

19. TREVOR LEE & OPIUM: BRINGING ASIAN FUSION FOOD TO THE DEAR GREEN PLACE ... 161

20. STEPHEN CRAWFORD: REGIONAL HEAD CHEF WITH SIX BY NICO; COMMITMENT, RESILIENCE & TALENT ... 167

21. FERRIER RICHARDSON: THE CELEBRITY CHEF COMES HOME ... 175

22. BRIAN SCANLAN: CAMERON HOUSE, ON THE BONNIE BANKS ... 187

23. AURELIEN MOUREZ: OX & FINCH, TAPAS WITH A DIFFERENCE ... 198

24. ASIF ALI: SHISH MAHAL, A GLASGOW INDIAN LEGEND ... 202

25. STEFANO GIOVANAZZI: CAFÉ PARMA, KEEPING A FAMILY TRADITION ... 209

26. MARIO GIZZI: DI MAGGIO'S AND THE REST, AN INDEPENDENT GIANT ... 217

27. BRIAN MAULE: FINE DINING AT ITS BEST ... 227

INTRODUCTION:

DINING TALES: SAVORY STORIES TASTY TALES

In the past forty years Glasgow has been transformed from a location off the tourist grid into a bustling modern city open and welcoming to all with a vibrant arts and leisure life. Nowhere has this transformation been more apparent than with the city's dining scene.

Glasgow's restaurants and diners have gone from an overwhelming focus on fish n' chips, chops and gammon steaks to serving a wide range of dishes that cater to all tastes. Walk down any of the city's main streets and you will see a variety of eateries appealing to all palates.

Dining Tales highlights some of the pioneers behind this culinary revolution. Here they speak candidly of how they built their businesses with many challenges and pitfalls along the way. Hospitality can be a merciless business and most of the contributors to *Dining Tales* have had to overcome adversity with great tenacity and resilience.

The contributors to *Dining Tales* comprise a rich variety. There are those, largely Scots Italian, who are the third or fourth generation from families who began from humble origins and through sheer hard work built their restaurants and cafes into brands whose names are instantly recognizable to most Glaswegians. Such names include Sarti, the Crollas and the Coias.

These families, described by a son of one of them, Domenico Crolla as a "gene pool of genius," have not only given the city great restaurants. Beginning with modest cafes selling fish suppers or ice creams, they've developed cateries which are constantly busy but also, as with the Coias and Celinos, have become hubs of their communities, accessible and welcome to all.

Then there are those who've worked their way up the industry to the most senior levels. People such as Brian Scanlan or Seumas McInnes, who started out as kitchen porters and are now executive head chefs or owners of their own restaurants. Or Gillian Eagleson who began as a waitress and became Scotland's first woman executive head chef and now runs her own successful bakery business.

We meet those such as Graeme Cheevers, Ryan James and Peter Mckenna who have played a major part in developing Glasgow's burgeoning fine dining scene over the past few decades with establishments such as *Unalome*, *The Buttery* and *The Gannet* which are now firmly part of the Glasgow culinary landscape.

We also meet two major players from Europe who've made their mark on the scene. Aurelien Mourez from France has revolutionized what is meant by 'fine dining' by cooking up innovative dishes at his *Ox and Finch* outlet while the inimitable Zoltan Szabo from Hungary has literally carved his way through the Scottish dining establishment, including producing and selling fresh and delicious food at his successful farm food outlet for a while.

No account of Glasgow's restaurant scene could possibly be complete without the contributions Chinese and Indian food have made to the broadening of the city's culinary horizon. Trevor Lee with *Opium* has opened new vistas for blending fusion dishes; we hear his remarkable story here. Or Asif Ali, third generation owner of the legendary *Shish Mahal* Indian restaurant whose father invented that most signature of curry dishes, masala. Asif recounts the background to that and a lot more.

Along the way our contributors tell of many funny and quirky episodes: from nearly incurring the wrath of gangsters, almost knocking back rock royalty, hosting international super stars, or benefiting, ironically, from terrible reviews and much more.

If there is one common factor that unites all our contributors, it is sheer hard work. Building, and more importantly, sustaining a successful restaurant, as will become graphically evident in the pages of *Dining Tales,* requires intensive commitment, resilience, and utter dedication. Running a restaurant is a lifestyle that goes well beyond nine-to-five.

One other strong theme that comes across from all the contributors is the skills set needed to work within a demanding and hectic environment. Overseeing a busy kitchen and a bustling front of house necessitates good people skills to get the best from staff, excellent timekeeping, co-ordination, and dexterity, as well as ensuring standards, quality and delivery are being upheld. None of the contributors in this book just walked into being an executive head chef or owner of a restaurant. They learned the hard way on the job, both in the kitchen and in front of house. And it is that invaluable experience which has allowed them to keep on top of their game. *Dining Tales* highlights the craft that goes into making a successful restaurant.

But it's not all hard work and stress. One of the other strong themes that emerges in the pages that follow is the tremendous satisfaction and wellbeing that derives from operating a successful and well-regarded restaurant. Yes, there's the prestige and rewards that come from that. But there are two further motivations that come across vividly in these testimonies.

Firstly, there is the sheer pleasure derived from serving people delicious food which they enjoy and will come back for more. And, secondly, the satisfaction of knowing you've made people happy, particularly on their special occasions such as that first date, or a birthday treat, an anniversary and so on. That satisfaction and reward outweighs all the stress and strain that comes with the job.

The contributors to *Dining Tales* are business people and senior managers as well as being head chefs and owners. But what comes across clearly is a strong commitment to service for their customers and the communities they come from. That is why their customers come back and why venues such as those highlighted here have endured in an industry otherwise noted for high turnover and short lives.

Dining Tales comprises the edited highlights of 27 interviews with a selection of leading chefs and restaurant owners in Glasgow. Most of the interviews were carried out by Marco Giannasi who transformed a dilapidated former tram halt into the hugely popular *Battlefield Rest* restaurant in Glasgow. The other interviews were carried out by Alex Meikle who has been a former CEO of several third sector social care organisations and is now a spy fiction writer.

Each chapter follows a standard format beginning with the background to how each contributor started out, the significant episodes in their journey, including setbacks, to where they are today and how they got there. Along the way they recall some funny, quirky, and often hair-raising stories. Finally, each chapter concludes with sage words of advice from the contributors to people thinking of coming into the restaurant business and concludes with each contributor revealing their favourite wine and favourite dish.

Whether you love food, eat out regularly or are interested in working in the restaurant business, *Dining Tales* is a fascinating insight into the ingredients and personalities of those extraordinary people who make great and enduring restaurants serving sumptuous food while making it seem all so easy to their customers.

Marco Giannasi
Alex Meikle
Glasgow December 2023

1. JOHN QUIGLEY: NO TEARS WITH THIS RED ONION

Situated in the heart of Glasgow city-centre, Red Onion run by chef and owner, John Quigley, has become a popular venue in the city serving new interpretations of classic Scottish cooking. John recounts the colourful journey that led to the Red Onion

Beginnings

Both my parents worked full-time and though they loved cooking, as a hard-working teacher and a nurse respectively, they had little time to do it in, so I started cooking for my family and six siblings. This was mainly simple food such as mince and tatties, bacon, eggs and chips. My grandparents were another huge influence on me as I was always hanging around their home watching them and helping out while they were making good, wholesome fresh food from simple ingredients. I remember distinctly faking asthma attacks so I could spend some days with my granny helping her to bake cakes, pies, bread, clootie dumpling etc.

In those days men were not encouraged to cook, it wasn't the culture. There were few opportunities locally in Scotland except for chefs working in the big hotels. I ended up in London and washed dishes.

I got to know a guy called Andrew Edwards who owned a small, bohemian wine bar in Soho. He was a brilliant wine expert, but rather eccentric. The bar had a limited menu which served mainly deli items. He gave me the opportunity to run the wine bar and I added to the menu by bringing some of my family's recipes – hotpots, stews and soups – to it. I steadily built up the bar's reputation and popularity. Within a few years, aged just 22, I became the youngest Head Chef to be listed in the *Good Food Guide* mainly thanks to my granny's soup!

On the road with the Rock n' Roll chef

After a few years I fancied a change. It was quite a radical change as I ended up on the road as a rock and roll touring chef working for a company called *Eat Your Hearts* out on Tina Turner's European Foreign Affairs tour when I was in my mid-to-late twenties. Initially, it was for six weeks but I ended up spending six months with her. It was crazy. Every day we were building a new kitchen in different venues, including arenas with different power sources. The conditions were variable, and we had to cook for a broad spectrum of palates from bacon and eggs to Chateaubriand. No day was the same and you could turn up at a venue with different kitchens and setup from the day before, the power sources could be different, and prior to the euro there could be a different currency. It was constantly changing and challenging.

We fed the truckers and roadies basic food such as bacon and eggs. The more sophisticated palates were higher up the chain. Tina, however, was no prima donna and ate the same food as the truckers and roadies.

There was a difference between the Mediterranean countries where you had to do everything on the day from scratch and the northern European countries where there was almost always a kitchen set up for you. I'll never forget once being in the middle of a bullring in sand with bits of a bull hanging up around me. Thankfully that's all changed now and the standards in southern Europe are the same as the north.

After Tina Turner, I worked with the Bee Gees. To be honest that was more sedate as the band toured with their families. In contrast, I also cooked on tour for Guns N' Roses, which was madness, and others including the late Whitney Huston.

Finally, I got a contract to work with Bryan Adams. He was a vegan and insisted his entire crew ate only vegetarian food which, to say the least, caused great dissatisfaction. He was about to sack the entire catering crew, but I was parachuted in to rescue the situation as I had a reputation for good vegan cooking. Ultimately Brayn retained me as his private chef and I stayed with him for five years, before, having cooked the world, I decided it was time to settle down and come back home.

Back in Glasgow. **The "style bars"**

The city had changed and there were more opportunities than before I'd left. I worked in one of the original "style bars", *Mojo* which was rather adventurous for Glasgow then. It was a different league, however, from cooking for one man to having to fire up forty burgers at a time; that was a steep learning curve! But the bars were heaving, the kitchens were buzzing, and they were a huge success. A bonus for me is that I met my future wife one evening in the bar at *Mojo*.

Following my growing reputation working in *Mojo*, I was head-hunted to work for the G1 Group and then to work for a new venue called the *Arthouse Hotel*. This was a massive success for about two years. The owners gave me a lot of freedom to do what I wanted. I installed the first teriyaki grill and sushi chef in Scotland. *Arthouse* became a massive success. We were serving 600 covers a day and had 36 chefs and catered to top drawer celebrities like Tom Cruise and Eminem in the house regularly. It was amazing while it lasted.

But after a fantastic first two years, things began going wrong. It was apparent that the business was not being run properly and it was time for me to move on.

I was then approached to become involved with opening a venue with my name above the door and so this became *Quigley's*. It was flattering to have a place named after me, even though I had no money invested in it, just my name, and whilst it was successful, the owners had plans to transform it into a nightclub, which didn't appeal and I thought now was the correct time to start my own business with my business partner and wife, Gillian.

Opening my own place

I noticed there was a property in town which was lying empty. It had been a restaurant previously owned by Gordon Yuill, a famous Glasgow restaurateur. One day I met the landlord when he was leaving the premises and he told me they were about to go on the market. I let him know I was interested in buying it and within eleven days I had the keys. I called it *Red Onion*. We're now in year twenty, and I've not looked back since. It's been a steady success.

How do you maintain that success? Well, as the owner I'm always on the floor and committed to the business. But I've also got a hardworking, friendly staff; most of the kitchen staff have been with me for 15-20 years which speaks for itself.

The food we serve is high quality, affordable and delicious and I place a strong premium on good customer service, which in turn attracts a loyal following.

We have a strong inclusive dining policy with a menu for everyone, but which also appeals to several niche markets. For example, you could have a family of four with one person wanting glutton free food, another can only have dairy free, the third is vegan and the last person could be glutton free *and* vegan. You need to accommodate all four and that's what we do at *Red Onion*; strive to meet the needs of all our customers. People appreciate that and families know they can come to our restaurant where everybody can be catered for.

I have been very proactive in promoting Glasgow as a tourist dining destination and have worked with the Glasgow Marketing Board at several large tourism expos in the UK promoting both the city and *Red Onion*. As a result, we have cultivated relationships with several international tour operators which of course brings a wide range of foreign visitors to the restaurant.

We have challenges all the time in this trade, no matter how long you've been in the business. For instance, in the summer of 2023 we were catering for the Summer Nights' concerts at the Bandstand in Kelvingrove, one of Glasgow's main parks. We had over 500 weights of food and a car boot full of food to deliver. The problem was the event was being held on the same weekend as the international UCI cycling finals in Glasgow, so all the roads were blocked off both at the venue and at the restaurant. We couldn't drive to it. So, we had staff in chain gangs pushing shopping trolleys along Sauchiehall Street to ensure the food was transported to the event. And we did it! The concertgoers were fed.

Recently, we had a coach party of French tourists and I mistakenly and stupidly put HP brown sauce on their ice creams! But they lapped it up and went away profoundly happy. There's a whole group of French tourists out there who believe we Scots love brown sauce with our ice cream!

I'm delighted *Red Onion* has been a success now for nearly two decades and become a feature of Glasgow city-centre dining. Long may it continue.

Advice

To succeed in this business, you must enjoy cooking every day. The moment cooking becomes a chore is the day to reconsider. The best advice I can give is to try and work in the right kitchen at the right time. I was fortunate in that I've worked in creative environments which helped to foster young talent and allow them to flourish. It's absolutely essential you have extensive experience of kitchens and cooking before taking on senior roles in this trade, not least if you're considering running your own restaurant.

John's favourite dish: Fresh food, well-seasoned and cooked. Simple food like my parents and grandparents made such as minestrone soup with ham hough or white sole with potatoes and cream just like my mother cooked.

John's favourite wine: Again, nothing extravagant, a new world Soave

*

2. GIOVANNA EUSEBI, EUSEBI DELI: EAST & WEST, FRESH IS THE BEST

Starting in Glasgow's east end Eusebi Deli has become renowned for serving wholesome fresh produce. Owner Giovanna Eusebi traces the background of this very popular deli and restaurant rooted in family, good wholesome cooking and serving the community.

Beginnings

My Grandparents lived a simple rural life in southern Italy. This shaped how I see and work with food. They grew all their own food sustainably which has hugely influenced my food story at the restaurant today.

My parents owned fruit shops and I grew up in that environment. My very first job was polishing apples for the fruit displays in the window, I could barely see over the counter. I was conscious that we had a different life from other children, for example, we didn't have family holidays as one parent always had to man the business; closing wasn't an option.

My family worked long hours. We rarely ate in restaurants, which is quite ironic given that we went on to own and run one. There was no eating a packet of crisps for breakfast on your way to school for us; we always had to eat at a table, and I did my homework in the back of the shops. To me all this was just normal. My parents provided me with that all-important real-life education.

An East-End Haven

Dad owned a deli in Shettleston in the east end of Glasgow where he was born and raised. I began working in my parent's shops when my son was about four, I gave up my job working for British Airways as I wanted to be home with my family. We were a small core team consisting of my father, mother and some lovely ladies including some relatives and friends. There was something beautiful about all these women kneading and hand rolling pasta each day while chattering together over the dull sound of the cranking Imperia machine. It was lovely and I have very fond memories of that period.

We heard reliable stories that local people were coming in, buying our pasta products, taking them home and pretending they'd made it themselves! That was never questioned by us, after all, as we would often say *what happens in Eusebi stays in Eusebi.*

The east end deli was often described as a beacon of light in an area that was tagged by the World Health Organisation as having the lowest life expectancy in Europe. It was renowned for its bad diet and not on the map as a culinary destination. I only ever experienced kindness and generosity of spirit. It may have seemed strange to find natural wines, buffalo mozzarella cheese and delicious ripe San Marzano tomatoes (this was the early 90's) in this setting and it felt more like an Italian hilltop grocers but in the east end of Glasgow.

On one occasion in 2008, the east end was home to a crucial by-election and there was an influx of journalists in the area to cover it. During the campaign on a typical day at the deli, my son, Nico, who was eight at the time was with me after school. I had made him a Dalek costume from an old cardboard box with a makeshift antenna from a loo roll strapped to his head. As he navigated the counter shouting 'exterminate, exterminate,' three journalists appeared. Two of them covered stories for the local Glasgow newspaper called the *Evening Times* and would often pop by if they were in the area. The third introduced himself as Adrian from London. He looked younger than his years, his sun kissed skin was smooth and his eyes were piercing blue. He was drop dead handsome and looked as if he had just stepped off a Giorgio Armani catwalk. I offered them espresso and a bite to eat. As you would expect, I was so proud of our produce waxing lyrical about the fresh delivery of San Marzano tomatoes and the cheeses which had been delivered that morning. Adrian opted for a sandwich with both Sardinian Pecorino and San Marzano cheese. He thanked me graciously and we chatted all things Italian before, as he was leaving patting Nico's head and shaking my hand. He was charming.

The next day I opened the *Times* (the London one) and saw an article with the headline: "Welcome to Glasgow's east end: the hardest, poorest place in Britain", he pulled no punches, and the piece was dotted with wicked anecdotes. He described Shettleston as "making the rough margins of Liverpool look like the Chelsea flower show." He spoke of visiting a local card shop, picking up a "happy 100th Birthday" greeting card and asking the girl behind the counter if she had ever sold one. He wrote that "she gives me a f**k off look and says 'no'." Predictable journalism perhaps, but the journalist, Adrian, was in fact A.A. Gill the famous London food critic.

He came back up to see us a few times and one of the journalists who was a regular at the deli informed me he loved the little shop and its hospitality. That story goes to prove the adage: you never know who's going to come through the door, so you must treat everyone the same, no matter who they are.

Another time in Shettleston, it was Halloween and dad was behind the counter, Dean Martin as ever playing in the background. The deli was mobbed, and he was cutting up hams when a customer came in and asked him:

'Who are you dressing up as tonight, Eddie?'

Dad was below the counter so, he popped his head up and said: 'the invisible man,' before ducking back down. That brought the house down.

I worked with my dad every day at the deli until he sadly passed away. I continued to run the deli, though it was tough without my father's guidance, but you must pick yourself up and get on with it, which is what I did.

Expanding to the West

My brother found a site in the West End close to Kelvingrove Park and we decided that we would open a restaurant alongside the deli. Even though we hadn't operated a restaurant before, we knew that food and hospitality were in our DNA. The new Eusebi opened eight years ago and has gone from strength to strength since.

We've built on our experience and skills acquired from running the deli in Shettleston and transferred that across to the West End. The place is buzzing and brilliant to be in. I'm delighted to say Eusebi in the West End is now on the map and operating successfully in a very competitive area and the key to that, as always, is good food, hard work, and consistency.

We've had our memorable little incidents in the West End venue too. The most remarkable for me was when a woman customer, having dinner, turned out to be the daughter of the iconic revolutionary Che Guevara! She was accompanied by a famous Cuban actor. They were both delightful and loved their food. She was a fabulous lady, and she even autographed a Eusebi shirt for me.

Advice and the delights and challenges of working in hospitality.

Hospitality for me is people coming in as customers and leaving as friends. It's about humanity at its kindest. You might have someone who's going through an illness, or a hard time and you must make their experience at dinner worthwhile and meaningful to them. Or there's the couple who are in love and the food, the service and atmosphere enhances and finishes everything off and makes that evening unforgettable. This is what you're doing; not just serving food, though, of course, that's important, but you're also creating a beautiful experience. It's truly vocational. I love seeing the reaction of people to their food, watching their body language; that is very fulfilling.

I prefer simple dishes. I remember with my grandmother that twenty people could turn up at her house and she would rustle up a fantastic meal from the simplest of ingredients using only a tiny wee simple cooker. Nowadays chefs are so lucky to have all the gadgets around them when really, no matter how much training you have, the techniques are always in your hands. That's everything. It's also vital that you care who you are cooking for. If somebody asks me: 'how do you make good Italian food?' I would answer: 'with simple ingredients and a whole lot of sentiment!'

I love the business, but it's a tiring job. You're on seven days a week and at the end of the day your body's sore and your feet are aching so, it's vital you switch off. I'm a lone wolf because everyone's wanting a part of you when you're in the restaurant; you can never switch off. I love nothing more than to sit with a good book in silence to relieve the pressure. That keeps you sane and motivated. But, just now, I couldn't imagine doing anything else. To see happy, satisfied customers leaving your premises makes it all worthwhile.

Giovanna's favourite dish:
My favourite dish is just a simple pasta with sugo washed down with:

Giovanna's favourite wine: A glass of Lugana. If anything, it's not really about what you're eating but who you are eating it with that elevates the simplest dish to a memorable dining experience.

3. SARTI: A GLASGOW ITALIAN JOURNEY

With two popular restaurants in the city, the Sarti family have carved out a good reputation for combining the finest Scottish ingredients with excellent Scottish produce to create and serve traditional and authentic Cucina Toscana and Liguria. Prominent family member, Sandro Sarti here outlines the colourful background to the family's success.

Beginnings
It really starts in 1912 when my great Grandfather suddenly died of pneumonia and my Nonno (grandfather)

had to leave Italy, to try to make some money so that his family could eat. He made his way to Cherbourg and boarded the White Star *Saint Paul* ship headed for New York. In the US he had been invited by his uncle to join him on a Pinto Bean plantation in Sacramento. But at the famous Ellis Island Centre outside New York, he was assessed to have a high temperature which they thought could be TB. Detained in what was effectively a prison on Ellis Island for six weeks until he was put on a ship sailing back to Europe, he ended back in Cherbourg in France where he'd started out from.

He felt cheated and defeated at this, but then remembered he had a cousin who owned a fish and chip shop in Scotland, Motherwell to be precise, and that's where he headed to. He met up with his cousin who gave him a job. Having no command of English back then, his job was to go to the fish market in Glasgow's Saltmarket in the early morning and pick the best fresh fish which he brought back to the shop in a special railway wagon.

They could have had the fish delivered from Glasgow, but his cousin knew that the fishmongers only delivered the older, lesser quality fish. It was far better that my Nonno selected and brought back the best fish. He hated the job but stuck it out as he was earning some money. In fact, he was able to send the princely sum of £1 a week to his family in Italy.

Eventually, they were able to buy premises next to the shop and opened a billiards hall. Those were tough times. Motherwell was a rough and tumble steel and coalmining town, and they were plenty of fights in the hall with glasses and heads being smashed.

At that time, you could only get products such as olive oil from places like Boots in tiny bottles. There was only a limited range you could source locally, and the quality wasn't great; it was not authentically Italian. This prompted my grandfather to send for his brothers and together they set up a small importing company and delivered to Italian families by bike with a sidecar. They started this business called *Fazzi*

Brothers to import the produce and act as wholesalers to the trade in the west of Scotland.

My father was born in Glasgow but returned to Italy when he was still a baby. He fought in the war for Italy in Albania and Yugoslavia and was taken prisoner by the Germans, at a munitions factory in Cologne where he endured many hardships. After the war and coming home to La Spezia, finding work was impossible so he travelled to Scotland and started working in one of his uncle's shops near the city centre at Anderston Cross.

Peaky blinders in post-war Glasgow, a rough city

It was a tough area with a lot of hard, mainly Irish gangs. My dad was involved in a few fights. But he could handle himself; he'd fought in the war, and he was well built and fearless. One time, two guys came into the shop demanding free cigarettes. Dad made it patently clear to them in his heavily accented English that there would be no free cigarettes. These guys then started smashing up the glass cases displaying the cigarettes and chocolates. Dad picked up a Knickerbocker Glory glass and smashed one of the guys in the face and cut one of his ears off. Seriously! Years later, I saw that guy working as a carpark attendant and he only had one ear! Another time a troublemaker wanted to fight and insulted Lucio by calling him a "tally bastard". Lucio punched him so hard that he went through the glass door, was scooped up by a passing tram and was carried as far as the Kelvingrove Art Gallery.

Another time, a gang of thugs descended on the shop, peaky blinders style, and menacingly announced: 'we're going to meet you at the tunnel between Argyle Street and St Vincent Street', where either my dad or his uncle would make their way to deposit the shop's takings in a nearby night safe, 'and we're going to take your money.'

Dad immediately went to some friends who had access to a sawn-off shotgun, clubs, razors and knuckle dusters. Tooled up, wearing bonnets on a foggy night, with long coats and carrying a leather case like something out of a Hollywood gangster movie, Dad, his uncle, and their accomplices, all cafe and chip shop owners, headed through the tunnel. Sure enough, at the other end waiting for them were the gang dressed in donkey jackets and armed with clubs with nails sticking out and crowbars.

There was a bit of a stand-off, but eventually the main guy, a fellow called 'Jimmy' declares:

'Your tough guys so are we. We're all living in the same place, and we can live together,' and they backed off. There was no further fighting or intimidation. Yes, they were tough times all right!

Learning the trade: don't spill coffee into a saucer and performing the conga.

I was brought up mainly by my nonna as my parents worked all the hours God sent. But they never spoke a word of English at home. When you stepped through our threshold you stepped into Italy. By the age of six I could still only speak Italian! I was sent to a posh primary school run by nuns in Pollokshields, the Nuns only interest in me was that they were determined I would become a priest! My folks took me out of there and eventually I ended up in Lourdes. No, not the holy water, miracle working town of Bernadette fame in France, but a Glasgow secondary school in Cardonald. A miracle of sorts did happen, I suppose, because my English rapidly improved and I did reasonably well for the rest of my time at school. I moved up onto another secondary school called Holyrood after my first year.

Leaving school, I got lured into the family business. *Fazzi Brothers* had become quite a substantial business. I liked the idea of becoming a salesman and *Fazzi' Brothers* had positions open for two travelling salesmen: one covering Glasgow north of the Clyde, the other Glasgow south of the Clyde. I covered the north side. It was a great time. I was a young guy with a car, decent clothes and travelling around the country living in great hotels.

Through my father, I also got a job at a popular and well-established Italian restaurant in Glasgow which supplemented my income as a salesman. This was *L'ariosto* owned by a certain Mr Giannasi (the father of Marco Giannasi of *Battlefield Rest* fame) who was friendly with my father.

It was hard work, but I learned a lot about cooking, catering and picked up a lot of kitchen skills that were invaluable experience for later while I worked in *L'ariosto*, though mostly I was a waiter there. But, of course, there were the inevitable faux pas. One day I was carrying three heavy plates, one of them containing a dish 'steak pizzaiola' with lots of sauce. Despite my best efforts, the sauce from the plate slurped onto a young lady's dress at the table. I went to a backroom with the young lady where the washing machine was located. She slipped out of the dress (I didn't look of course), put it in the washing machine and we managed to get it dried and clear of all the stains. Wow!

Mr Giannasi was quite a stickler. For example, he abominated coffee spilling onto a saucer. If he saw a waiter about to serve coffee like that, he would blow a gasket. One day there was a young Italian waiter, it was about his second day on the job. The restaurant was very busy with a whole host of local personalities such as the TV presenter, Bill Tennant. The young chap carried four cups at a time and confidently swaggered towards the table. Some of the coffees spilled onto the saucers. Mr Giannasi noticed this and ordered the young chap: 'Back!'. So, the hapless waiter goes back to the counter where his poor colleague had to make up all the cappuccinos afresh. The young waiter collected them again and once more quickly headed back to the table. However, the coffee spilled again and Mr Giannasi, watching the waiter like a hawk now, ordered him back once more. The young waiter, exasperated, threw the cups in the air and they shattered on the ground before storming out showering the nearby customers in cappuccino, We never saw him again.

It was hard work, but there were some great times in *L'ariosto*. I remember at Christmas time; a lot of the women would get very tipsy and make up a row to perform the conga. We were ordered to join in, and we would end up leading a conga following the group headed by Toni Capaldi and his quartet up and down the Mitchell Street car park to the bemusement of passers-by. It was wintertime with ice or snow on the ground and we would be slipping and sliding up and down the car park slopes wearing patent black shoes while attempting to lead this conga with a highly refreshed bevy of women. You couldn't make it up!

I was working Monday to Friday at *Fazzi Brothers* during the day and waiting in *L'ariosto* at night. I always took Saturdays off as that was the only time, I could see my girlfriend. One evening in the restaurant, Mr Giannasi called me over.

'Sarti,' he addressed me in typical Italian fashion by my surname, 'Saturday night is the busiest night in the restaurant business. We cannot let you have that night off.'

I replied, sorry, but that was the only night I was able to see my girlfriend. So, I got fired; the only time in my life I have been fired.

Back at *Fazzi Brothers*, we purchased the Capaldi Italian grocers shop then moved to the corner site at Cambridge Street at the north side of the city-centre. We decided to make a third of the shop into a café with a small, basic menu. *Fazzi Brothers* thought they would make a foray into dining. It turned out to be very successful. They also opened another restaurant in the affluent Glasgow suburb of Newton Mearns.

It all went well at first but the business model of paying commissions to salesmen and travellers for the product side of the business wasn't really keeping up with the times and for various reasons *Fazzi Brothers* folded. It wasn't helped by the fact that the various arms of the business were under one name, so when one part failed the entire enterprise went down like a pack of cards. If the different parts had been under different company names, it might have survived. But that's hindsight or a bad accountant for you!

Incidentally, *Fazzi* kept a "strange request book" from customers that included such gems as: "the hole in my expresso cup was too small for my finger." Or: "Really annoyed that I've been waiting seven minutes for my Spaghetti!"

The rise of Sarti

After *Fazzi Brothers* went under, my brother, Piero, and I, decided we would open our own boutique osteria and after some haggling with an estate agent, we found this little place on Wellington Street and opened *Sarti* in 1991. At that time there was only one other restaurant in the vicinity. It was an immediate success, even though we had a limited menu at that time. We were busy morning, noon and night and had queues snaking along Wellington Street and up neighbouring West George Street as we didn't take bookings. Shortly after, we opened another place in Bath Street just round the corner. These were both good times in that we were making lots of money, but also bad times because we didn't see much of our families.

In 2000 we opened in the city centre, at Renfield Street. Unfortunately, busy and successful though that restaurant was, it didn't survive covid. But Sarti has still got the two neighbouring restaurants in Bath Street and Wellington Street and the area around them is now popular for nightclubs and restaurants. My daughter Daniela now runs the restaurants with her team.

The two restaurants are separate but are connected by passageways and tunnels so staff and sometime customers can move between the two. Indeed, there's a possibility that the restaurants may be haunted.

A ghost in the loo!

Personally, I've never seen anything, but I was witness to a weird and scary incident. One night I was closing the restaurant and noticed that the staff toilet downstairs was locked. It can only be opened from the inside by a six-inch bolt, so before closing the restaurants I knocked on the door and shouted: 'Hurry-up, we're going soon,' and went back upstairs. When I arrived there, to my surprise, all the staff were having a wee drink after a busy day as is standard in restaurants. I thought nothing further about it and went home.

Next morning at 7am, the manageress phoned, quite alarmed, to say the downstairs toilet was locked. I thought, 'oh my God, have we left someone stuck in there?' 'I told her to wait until the chef came in. Eventually the chef kicked the toilet door open and…there was no one there! Yet it could only be opened from the inside. Spooky!

Ever since in that toilet the ballcock seems to switch itself on and off by itself. There's a switch that does this, but it must be operated manually, otherwise as the plumber we brought in pointed out toilets 'don't switch themselves off and on their own, otherwise the whole of Glasgow would be at a stop!' We also seem to have a poltergeist on the premises with pieces of paper sometimes scattered on the floor when we open in the morning.

In the staff section, it is said that you can sometimes hear at midnight the sound of a cradle rocking and a man sobbing. I've never heard anything myself, but the story is attributable apparently to an admiral who once lived in the building who came back after fighting in some war in Italy and was devastated and broke down in tears when told by his wife that their baby had died. Many Glasgow restaurants do seem to have an affinity to the supernatural.

I'm delighted that *Sarti* has become a feature in Glasgow. It's been quite a journey to get here, and it wouldn't have happened at all if the Americans hadn't knocked my nonno back!

Mind you, I wish I was there with my nonno when he stood on the quay at the port back in France and said: 'I'm going to Motherwell,' and I could have said to him: 'Could we not make it California nonno?

Advice

For people thinking of going into the catering or the hospitality trade I would say this business can give you lots of satisfaction, you get to meet lots of interesting and famous people, including a few rogues and just great genuine people. There is nothing better than when a customer is happy and complements your food and staff.

On the downside, it is very, very hard work with terrible unsociable hours. In my career I've kissed my children in the morning when they were still in bed, gone out to work and not seen them again until I've kissed them at night when they were back in bed. Piero and I have always tried to take two days off a week, and they were precious days spent as much as possible with the family.

Don't go into the restaurant trade with eyes wide open, it's not easy, especially nowadays where there is a huge choice and not enough people to go round. Make sure you have a great idea for your restaurant, think carefully about where you would like to open; just because you're located in the city-centre does not guarantee success.

Keep your menus simple, in Italy menus are simple and do not have a huge selection. Simple menus will save you money on stock and wastage. Also change your menus seasonally.

If I were younger I would probably open other restaurants and always follow closely what is trending in Italy, never depending on or copying what is currently fashionable in the UK. Remember everything has a shelf life, so don't copy what you think is a dead certainty because it's busy now, it might not be in a year.

My final comment on this would be once you get the restaurant bug it's impossible to shake it off!

Sandro's favourite dish:

As Piero and I have been in the restaurant all of our lives and cooked almost everything, it's difficult to pinpoint one singular dish. As most chefs will tell you after service what we crave is comfort food.

If I had to choose one dish that I really love, it would be a nice plate of Tordelli Lucchesi in a rich beef Ragù. Tordelli ("little thrushes") is a coarse pasta, stuffed with a rich beef, salsiccia, Parmigiano, egg, nutmeg and lots more stuffing. Served with a rich beef Ragù. In Italy its wise to order this as a "piatto unico" a single dish as its very filling, followed by some lovely Italian cheese. A nice red wine would accompany this dish perfectly.

Sandro's favourite wines:

Either a lovely Chianti Classico or Morellino di Scansano, Fubbiano Rosso, not forgetting a Vino Nobile di Montepulciano.

4. THE STORY OF THE COIA'S: FOUR GENERATIONS OF A DINING LEGEND

For nearly a hundred years the Coia family have ran a popular café-cum-restaurant in Glasgow's east end which has become a focal point for the local community it serves. Alfredo Coia, the latest owner, recounts the family's incredible story.

Beginnings

My immediate family never had any intention of opening a café or anything like that. My grandfather was good with his hands and opened a shopfitting business called C & C Coia Corp. He fitted out a lot of cafes in Glasgow such as the *Burnside Café* and the famous *University Café* on Byres Road. A lot of these cafes are still around with their distinctive décor built by my grandfather in the 20s and 30s.

It was only in the late 1920s that my grandfather decided they were going to open a café called *Coia's Café* in Duke Street which, I think, is still one of the longest streets in Europe connecting parts of the east end of Glasgow to the city-centre. It's a very busy street with a large and vibrant community surrounding it. *Coia's Café* opened in 1928 and my grandfather fitted it out too.

The cafe sold ice creams, sweets and cigarettes and built a good and loyal customer base right through the 1920s and up until the Second World War.

My uncle, Alfredo, who I was named after, was called up to the army and sent to Palestine, now Israel, after the War. There was a lot of trouble in the area involving British troops trying to quell a big rebellion. One day he was sunbathing, and a sniper fired on him. He was shot and killed at the age of 21. He was buried in Tel Aviv in 1946. My grandparents only found out about his death by telegram.

It was expected that when Alfredo came home from the army, he would run the shopfitting business. But when he died my grandparents gave the business up.

Building the business: dad takes over.

My father, Nicky, like so many Scots Italians, was interred at the start of the Second War on the Isle of Man. Like my grandfather before him, he was good with his hands, and carved out this incredible wooden crucifix while he was interred which he gave to my grandmother. It's been handed down to me and I'm immensely proud of it.

Later, like his brother, he was also conscripted into the army for his national service. He wanted to serve abroad, but I suppose after what happened to her other son, my grandmother put her foot down and he was only posted to Edinburgh Castle; that was his tour of the world!

Any leave he had, he was working in the café and when he was demobbed, he went straight into working full-time there. My dad's influence in the café was also huge. Along with his wife, Gustinea, he turned it from an ice cream parlour into more of a snack bar. He brought in a juke box and moved it onto another level. It served basic food such as sausage, eggs and chips as well as adding some Italian food including minestrone soup and catered for everybody in the local community. It became even more popular all through the 1950s, 60s and 70s. I think it's safe to say that *Coia's* café became a local fixture, and my dad played a huge part in creating that.

When I look back, I realise that people like my grandmother and father laid the foundations for what we've got now. They worked bloody hard and provided a service to the community. A lot of their customers became friends. I still get people coming in the café to this day saying to me: 'I went to school with your dad.' Or 'I used to see your dad every day and he would serve me this or that,' or they would know my mother and the family. Your conscious of that heritage and tradition and keeping that legacy going as best you can.

The son's turn but avoid alienating gangsters.

I was very close to my father; in fact, he was more like a brother to me, and I went to the same school as he had. From an early age, I was immersed in the work of the café. I would have my lunch there and watch all the hustle and bustle going on. When I came home from school, my dad would have chores for me to do around the place such as stacking shelves and other tasks.

I remember once we used to sell these exotic cigars which were quite popular. One day there was a queue waiting outside the door. My father popped his head out to check the length of the queue and noticed this guy right at the end, in his fifties and quite distinguished looking. The man saw my father, put his hands up and shouted: 'I'm just here to pick up cigars.' Dad replied sharply to him: 'Well, wait your turn.'

Someone overheard this and later informed my dad: 'That was Arthur Thomson you told to wait.' This name meant nothing to either my father or me at the time and the guy did wait patiently and bought his cigars. It was only later that we discovered Arthur Thomson was one of Glasgow's most notorious underworld figures! Aye, and dad told him to wait his turn!

I wanted to work in the business when I left school and I studied for a Diploma in Hotel & Kitchen Management at college. Then I worked as a chef in Stirling before moving down to London and working as a commis chef in various places. I learned a lot from these jobs. Kitchens were very different places then from what they are now. They were very regimented and if the chef told you to jump, you jumped!

When I came back to Glasgow in the 1990s, I had a vision for the café. My wife and I wanted to expand it, turn it more into a restaurant without changing its heart in the community. Antonia, my wife has a great knowledge and feeling for Italian food which really added to the development of the business. We opened a new place just along the road from the existing café and kept the two businesses going for a few years until we gave the old premises up as it was under threat of a compulsory purchase order from the Council.

Following that we bought another site nearby we turned into a café/restaurant, though we didn't have an alcohol license. Both sites were busy and ticking along nicely. But then the opportunity arose to take on the premises *Coia's* currently operates from. Previously, it had been three units, was in a state of disrepair, and lay empty for a few years.

Then, in 2006, my wife and I were approached by the company constructing a new building on the site. They inquired if I was interested in taking on the bottom unit as they were building flats above. I looked over it and thought this was a good opportunity. So, I bought it and consolidated the two premises into one unit transforming it into a café/diner and restaurant combined.

Since it opened, Antonia and I have never looked back. I obtained a drinks licence and it's been incredibly busy. I feel with the restaurant I've taken the business to yet another level, building on the solid foundations laid by my father and my grandmother, but developing and enhancing it.

Keeping all customers happy

However, there were some reservations about the new style of *Coia's* not least from my "semi-retired" father. When we opened the new site, my dad, who'd just recently retired, came in and looked around this lovely new place his son had designed and put his head in his hands, saying:

'What have you done? You're going to lose all the customers. It's too fancy!'

I looked straight at him and said: 'Don't worry, dad, this will work.' But he persisted.

'What about the guy who comes in for his rolls in the morning; he'll not come in.'

'Yes, he will, dad, he'll still come in and we'll get other types of customers as well. It'll all fit together.'

I hate to say it, but I was right. We've not alienated the old customers, but we've broadened the clientele. So, we've still got people buying their rolls, but also people eating langoustines, clams, and scallops because people's palates and tastes have expanded so much. The point is we've managed to attract a broad base of customers. I'll give you an example.

After the new restaurant had opened, one night just after nine in the evening, an old customer, who's face I recognised and hadn't seen for a while, came in and took a table by himself. I served him and realised he had a drink in him as I took his order. He wasn't out of order or falling all over the place; just merrily tipsy. He ordered fish, chips and peas *and* a bottle of Crystal champagne which is a blend of Pinot Noir and Chardonnay.

As I said, he was an old customer, a local man, not shabbily dressed by any means, but dressed casually. The last thing I expected was for him to order a full bottle of Crystal champagne. Whisky, gin, beer even, but champagne! The guy registered this on my face and said bluntly to me:

'Do you think I've not got the money?' and produced a wad of notes from his wallet.

'I never said that' I hastily replied to him and proceeded to serve him. He sat there on his own peacefully, ate his fish and drank a whole bottle of Crystal.

Two points about that story. One, never judge a customer by their appearance, and two, as I said to my father, we'll keep our customers, and they'll adapt to the new setting with us. That guy proved my point. We get everyone from all walks of life now.

We've never looked back since opening the new restaurant. At first, I worked mainly in the kitchen; front of house was secondary. If I'm being honest, I preferred the kitchen, I was more at home there. But you can't see your customers back there. So, I started walking the dining floor more.

I became overwhelmed as the business became more popular because everyone wants more of your time. I realised I needed a head chef because I couldn't do it all on my own. I was micromanaging the place. Now, I've brought in a brigade of chefs and three managers with different duties and responsibilities. I'll be honest, I still find it difficult to delegate and you need to be careful that you don't end up in the silly situation where people are inhibited from making decisions or acting on something because 'Alfredo will want to do that' and you're back to square one with everything left to you. I've slowly learned to disengage and let other people take charge, but as any proprietor will tell you, it's difficult but I'm getting there.

Focusing on the front of house has worked. I'm pleased with what we've achieved. I've greatly expanded our range of dishes and we're selling very high-quality wines. The business is now run by my wife, my son Carlo and myself. But this business never rests. You've constantly got to be alert to what's happening around you and work with that.

The impact of covid and the future.

We closed for the first couple of weeks of lockdown back in 2020, but we couldn't sustain that, and we started serving takeaways. We created an online platform and delivery service with the help of my son, Carlo, the next generation. That kept us going. The problem was when we fully reopened after lockdown ended, we were struggling to cope with both takeaways and normal table customers.

Even now, several years later, the pressure on the kitchen from a combination of Friday and Saturday night customers in the restaurant and the demand for takeaways can be enormous. Those chefs and that kitchen take a lot, and I don't want them to snap. We need to take a step forward to safeguard the future for *Coia's*.

There's a site nearby that's being redeveloped into houses, flats, and shops. A couple of years ago the Council approached me about this development and offered me a unit. I was interested but when I discovered that it was for rent, I told them 'no.'

But I really needed the space because we're bursting at the seams in the restaurant. I needed room for the take-aways, and I could only really achieve that on a separate site with a second kitchen. I went direct to the company building the development and told them I would be interested in acquiring a unit there, but only to purchase not to rent. They hummed and hawed but eventually they came back to me, and we agreed a deal.

The plan is to move all the takeaway business to the new site with a second kitchen. That will free up the restaurant and give me a bigger space. It will also take the heat off the guys in the kitchen who can focus now on the customers in the restaurant while the takeaways are being dealt with at the other site.

But there's another bonus. Currently, if people are early for their tables, but their table isn't free, but I know it will be within the next fifteen minutes, I've no place to put those customers. With the extra space I can create a bar/waiting area where people can sit, have a drink while their table's getting ready. Its win-win.

We are really excited about this new phase in the life of what will be, in a few years' time, a one-hundred years' old local institution. I'm so proud of that but also respectful of my grandmother, my mother and my father who built this business.

Advice

What advice would I give to people coming into this business? You need to love it and want to do it. Really put your heart into it. If you're doing it for a hobby or just to make money, it won't work. Hospitality and dealing with the public are a partnership. You need to understand people and just because you've got an idea doesn't guarantee success. A hospitality business needs a heart.

I've no disrespect for multiple chains; some of them do well, but they can lose heart. What you need is a winning combination of hard work, commitment, enthusiasm, and the ability to adapt to changing circumstances, all underlined with a good heart. For me, that's the best recipe to succeed in this game.

Alfredo's favourite dish: Turbot

Alfredo's favourite wine: Puglia Santini

5. DOMENICO CROLLA: A LICENCE TO SERVE PIZZA

A scion of one of Glasgow's most famous dining dynasties Domenico Crolla outlines his fascinating journey to running one of Glasgow's most successful pizzerias.

Beginnings
I've grown up in this business, starting in my father's restaurant, *La Costiera* in Glasgow city centre. I was 10 years

old when I started working in the cloakroom before, at 16, moving on to behind the bar. That early experience gave me some idea how the business worked.

I noticed there were different managers with different styles. For example, there was the legendary Tony Valenti who, for me, appeared incredibly suave, smooth, and sophisticated. I remember he would always kiss the women's hands. (He certainly wouldn't be doing that now!) Tony went on to run the Culinary Academy in Naples before retiring, but, to me, he summed up that old school charm.

Recently, I managed to find on Google an old menu from *La Costiera* dating back to 1980. The table d'hote was £1.80! Remarkably, there were no Italian dishes. The starters were either prawn cocktail, grapefruit, fruit juice or pate while the mains were the likes of steak Diane or peppercorn steak.

I think the reason for this was that the original Italians who came over here were not restaurateurs. Rather, they were just fortunate geniuses who got into the business and blagged it. Then along came outfits like Pizzaland, Pizza Express and the likes of Jamie Oliver and these guys started to think, particularly about Oliver, that: 'God, he's more authentically Italian than us.' He was using ingredients like mozzarella and sundried tomatoes.

Allied to this our customers were going on cheap Ryan Air flights to Italy, coming back and demanding what they'd seen and eaten there. We all had to pull our socks up. Change or die as they say. The upshot was we had to make our menus more authentically Italian.

The legendary *Dinos*

Dinos in the heart of town in Sauchiehall Street was a kind of midway point between the old-style Italian restaurants and the new, more authentic type. It was incredibly popular, and people saw it as genuinely Italian. My father bought it and it continued to be a runaway success.

It was always busy. At this stage my brother and I regarded ourselves as "sophisticated entrepreneurs". The two of us wanted to change everything in *Dinos* and we would cast a critical eye as my father worked there. I remember once we were watching my father making coffee and we started criticising how he was making it. He let us finish, then asked: 'How many kilos of coffee are you two selling each week?' We mentioned a figure and he replied, puffing on his cigar: 'I'm selling…' and quoted an amount many times greater. That ended the conversation. What's the old saying: If it's not fixed, don't try to mend it!

But the problem with *Dinos*, for all its success and popularity, was that it was too big and just too busy, as my dad latterly became aware. That sounds a bit daft; how can you be "too busy?" The problem was, it was so busy we couldn't get decent staff to work there. The waiters weren't great, in fact they were quite a grumpy bunch, and the chefs were mediocre. True, people thought the food was great. The reason for that was down to good ingredients. If you give the best chef in the world bad ingredients, he's not going to do a good job. However, even a mediocre chef will serve reasonably, tasty food with good produce.

When I my father ran *Dinos* he bought in only the best olive oil, beef and so on. It was all good quality products. And the place became a great meeting point, a Glasgow institution. When my father decided to close it in 2014, the reaction was incredible. Indeed, at one time he was reconsidering his decision to close, though he stuck by it. Nevertheless, people's emotional response to its closing was amazing. Dad held a sale of *Dinos* memorabilia such as t-shirts, aprons and the like which were snapped up eagerly. I'm very aware there are loads of people in Glasgow who have fond memories of *Dinos*.

Opening pizzerias and clashing with the chains

Long before then, I'd opened my first unit in a district of Glasgow called Cardonald on the southwest of the city. I called it *Domino's* which had absolutely nothing to do with the chain of that name because they weren't then operating in Europe. Ironically, I was inspired by the name when I went on holiday to Florida some 37 years ago. I came across this place called *Domino's* with the three dominos logo, looked through the window and saw it was a pizzeria. For me, it was the most beautiful, cleanest, gleaming pizzeria I'd ever seen up till then.

Back in Scotland, this inspired me to turn my unit into a a pizzeria and call it *Domino's Pizzeria*.

At the same time, another Scots Italian named Tony Arcari had just opened this beautiful chip shop not far from me. I thought, initially, this could be a threat as Tony had a bigger budget and a larger menu than me. So, I knew I had to focus on what I could do well which was making pizzas and with a limited budget try and source the best quality flour, tomatoes and so on that I could afford. In those days pizzas in Glasgow were all the same. It didn't take much effort to make your pizzas that bit tastier and more appealing to draw in the customers. Tony and I made a good trade and a decent living from our outlets.

That rolled along well for three years until I got this letter from a lawyer in Manchester ordering me to cease trading as I was in breach of copyright for using another business's name without permission. That business was *Domino's* who were now trading in the UK. There was no internet then and it took my lawyer a good five days to establish that they were a big outfit with access to lots of cash and I better comply. I changed the name to *Dom's Pizza*.

However, I have the pleasure of knowing that I had opened the first ever *Domino's* in the UK and at awards ceremonies I still can't resist approaching the table reserved for *Domino's* and letting them know that. I love watching their reaction and their eyes opening wide.

Mixing James Bond and gold pizza

In 2006 I bought a unit in Shawlands on Glasgow's Southside called *Bella Napoli*. At the same time, I was taking part in a pizza and pasta contest in London. Pizza has always been my passion and I really wanted to win the best pizza award. For me, it was an adventure and if I won, it would be fantastic publicity for my new venture.

As a sideline, I also decided to enter the pizza as an auction on eBay for charity. When I get excited about something I tend to go overboard, and this contest was no exception. I was absolutely determined to win it. There were five chefs, including myself, in the competition and I was confident I'd win it.

I flew down to Heathrow and on the taxi journey into London I noticed all these billboards advertising Daniel Craig showing off his body for his first Bond movie, *Casino Royale*. Those billboards and his face were everywhere as we drove in, and I noticed that the date for the premier of the movie was the same date as the pizza and pasta awards and the contest for best pizza. I got the inspiration to name the pizza I was going to cook for the competition, *Pizza Royale,* after the movie and to tie-in with the launch.

I decided I was going to put the most exotic ingredients into that pizza such as Beluga caviar, the finest salmon and sprinkle goldleaf over the pizza.

To extract the maximum publicity, I phoned a PR agent in Glasgow and told him I was going to win this competition in London. He interrupted me sharply: 'How are you so certain that you're going to win it?' I replied: 'Trust me, I will.'

I went on to tell him I was making the world's most expensive pizza. That just came out of my head, I hadn't planned to say that, and I listed the exotic ingredients I was going to use for the pizza. He didn't seem in the least impressed and asked:

'What's the angle here? There's nothing for the papers to get their teeth into.'

Then I mentioned the Bond angle and the tie-in with the launch of *Casino Royale*. That changed everything. I had his attention, and I could hear his mind whizzing. Then he said: 'Ok, I've got the angle now!'

I won the contest; but the PR guy was only interested in the Pizza Royale aspect. The story was syndicated around the world. Today we'd say it had gone viral. Within days I was getting calls from all around the world: Brazil, Australia, Hong Kong. All wanting to know about the world's most expensive pizza.

And it was. It sold at the auction for an incredible £2,150!

After that, the International Pizza Exposition in Las Vegas invited me to compete at their event and I was also asked to be part of a delegation of Italian pizza chefs demonstrating their skills in Hong Kong and so on. It opened door after door and was the best publicity I could ever have hoped for my new venture at *Bella Napoli*.

Changing with the times

The restaurant has been a great success. Despite this, in 2017 I decided to change the name. Many people, not least my staff and customers were puzzled: why? The reason was, there were now a few places in Glasgow which had opened with the name Bella such as *Bella Pasta*, *Bella Vita,* and a few others. More and more people were booking online and if they typed "Bella" into Google or Facebook there was a fair chance one of these other Bellas would pop up and we could end up losing out as a result.

I changed the name to *Oro*, which is Italian for coins or jewellery made from gold. It also gave me the excuse for another PR campaign. We announced the change and publicised it three months in advance. I'm glad we did so because, soon after, we were hit by Covid and the cost-of-living crisis. In that context, I'm glad that I changed the name to one that was distinctive and couldn't be mistaken for another brand.

Adaptation and change are the key to this game. There are two types of restaurateurs. Those – the geniuses I call them – who have the skills and wit to adapt and change. And those who inherited a restaurant from their family, think they know how to run it and believe that as long as they keep doing this, they'll be ok. But then everything changes around them, and they just can't adapt, and the upshot is lights out and closed doors.

Some years ago, I was speaking to a restaurateur whose business had went down. He was genuinely and sincerely baffled as to why and he said to me: 'I don't understand. I've done nothing different. I've changed nothing!' And that's probably why his place is no more.

Even before Covid things were changing in the restaurant business. People are cooking less and relying on eating out more. But because of that, they know more about food and they're expecting higher quality food.

Think of how fast things changed during the pandemic. I remember at the start of lockdown, supermarkets such as Waitrose were offering home deliveries, but because of the demand their app was offering delivery slots, sometimes up to a week later. People accepted it because of the novelty and the emergency.

But as time passed and people become more familiar with it, they started demanding a delivery the same day The supermarkets had to adapt and any who are still taking over a week to deliver will go under.

I never thought my business would do home deliveries. How could I possibly cope with a Saturday night crowd and doing home deliveries? But, after lockdown and people becoming accustomed to us doing takeaways, I knew it had become a necessity and we had to continue with it.

To adapt and cope, I've had to take certain things off the menu that take longer to cook and serve, lasagne for instance. It takes too long and is not fast enough. The need to turn tables is imperative. Being fully booked will pay your bills, but you get nothing back after that. It's the second and maybe third sittings that'll give you a decent living; that's the cream.

The key is to work out how to speed things up. In *Ora* I've taken the decision to stop taking bookings for big tables. The maximum booking now is for six people. Without big tables we find that turnaround is faster. People can sit in big tables for up to three or four hours and they don't necessarily spend more which means you're not earning more. In addition, big parties can often be loud and off-putting for other diners.

The 'gene pool of genius.'

When I look back, it's amazing how many characters who've came from Italy have established themselves as restaurateurs in this city. I call it a gene pool of genius. The places they've built up and the standards they've maintained have been really high, probably higher than London or Edinburgh I would argue. Just look at the number of times Glasgow Italian restaurateurs and chefs win national UK wards for Italian cuisine.

Part of this I think is to do with the fact that, internationally, Glasgow is still not a major tourist city, certainly not on the scale of London or Edinburgh. Think of Edinburgh during the Festival. It's absolutely mobbed. In that context, you don't have to try hard, in fact you can often get away with serving rubbish and it doesn't matter if people don't come back; there's so many to replace them. Same in London. In Glasgow, we don't have that scale so there's no incentive to serve rubbish. You've got to up your game to keep your customers.

It's an incredibly stressful business. There are times when I walk into my restaurant with a smiley face as it's fully staffed and fully booked and I've got my family, son and daughter, working beside me. It all's going well. And all it takes is for one member of staff not to show up and you're in for a roller-coaster of a night.

The worst is if your kitchen porter, the KP, doesn't turn up. The KP is probably the most important person after the chefs, because if a barman or waiter phones in sick someone else can cover. Not so with a KP. The chef or the head waiter aren't going to do the dishes, which is why I always pay the KPs a bit more.

Despite that, I've enjoyed my time in the trade. I've been forty years in this business, but I'm still sure I could do it better! I'm learning every day, as you should do.

Advice

Advice I'd give to people wanting to start up in the business? It's very tough currently, but it can be enjoyable and highly rewarding. In order to have a chance of succeeding you need to very adaptable, prepared to withstand a lot of stress and work very hard. Good luck.

Domenico's favourite dish: Pizza. I've had a passion for pizza ever since my mother at home would cook pizzas with homemade bread in front of the fire and I could see the loafs rising and the smell of yeast and flour assailing my senses. There was no mozzarella cheese available then, so she would simply sprinkle grated cheddar cheese over the pizza, melt the cheese and serve. It was the most wonderful dish I've ever tasted.

Domenico's favourite wine: It's probably heresy for someone of Italian descent and working in the restaurant trade to say this but I've never been a great wine lover. I used to love Asti Martini. It was very sweet and affordable. I remember on our honeymoon the hotel had put a bottle of Moet in our bedroom for us. I sent it back and demanded an Asti Martini!

Nowadays my sugar levels and tolerance are not what it was, so I prefer a good champagne from France.

6. MICHELE PAGLIOCCA: NEVER A DULL MOMENT IN THE TEAROOMS

Michele has been appointed by the Italian Government as the Honorary Consul to Scotland for Business Efficiency and assisting Italian citizens in Scotland who find themselves in poor circumstances.

From pub manager to nightclub owner, from running tearooms to hosting Prince and entertaining the Gallagher Brothers, Michele Pagliocca has seen and done it all. Here is his rollercoaster story.

Beginnings

When I was a young man in my teens back in the early 1970s, I wasn't the best behaved. My mother was in despair with me. I had a cousin who lived with his wife in Scotland. They'd previously owned a couple of cafes in Glasgow which they'd sold and now owned a petrol station and a café in Balmaha, a small town on the shores of Loch Lomond in a lovely, rural part of Scotland that attracts a lot of tourists. My mother took the opportunity, in the summer of 1972, to send me to Scotland to work at my cousin's petrol station and learn English.

I took to it like a duck to water and stayed for three years working at the petrol station. I picked up the language the best way you can, dealing with the locals and the tourists. However, after three years, my cousin decided to sell up and move back home.

I wanted to stay in Scotland and found a job in a classic Glasgow city centre pub called the *Burns Howff* which is long closed but has a legendary status in Glasgow pub history. It was a rock pub with bands playing virtually every night.

In a short space of time, I went from a petrol pump attendant in a nice, twee tourist village to working in a busy Glasgow pub. Fifty years ago Glasgow pubs were very different from what they are now. The *Burns Howff* wasn't exactly spit and sawdust, but not far from it. I learned the ropes at the pub from a gay barman called Alec who I watched very carefully. One day two guys came in and ordered two pints of lager. As he poured their pints and served them, I could hear them saying: 'he's gay, that bar man, he's f*****g gay.'

Back then homosexuality was illegal in Scotland and people like Alec had no comeback; he was on his own. But that didn't deter him. The two guys were getting louder, and Alec just turned round at the bar and ordered them out. They argued back. Then, to my astonishment, Alec jumped the bar, banged their heads together and threw them out! I'd never seen anything like that before.

A young barman in Glasgow

The manager of the *Burns Howf* was a Mr. Waterson, who became my father-in-law. He bought a place across the road called the *Whitehall*. This was a large venue and he turned it into a restaurant called *Olivers* and a cocktail bar, *Pat's Bar*, named after a barman, called Pat Melvin, who Mr Waterson had hired as he was then Scotland's best cocktail barman. Through Pat I learned how to make a huge variety of cocktails. Later this site was converted into three separate bars and nightclubs called *Kokomo*, *Bamboo* and the *Maltman* which are still there.

After a while, Mr. Waterson received an offer from Alfredo Crolla, a prominent Italian Glasgow restaurateur to buy part of the *Whitehall* which he was going to call *La Costiera*.

This became a very popular place, but Mr. Crolla had a definite idea about how he wanted to run the bar, especially after Pat Melvin retired. He brought in a couple of Italian guys to run it while I was sent upstairs to take charge of the restaurant.

However, things didn't go to plan with the bar downstairs and Mr. Crolla called me into his office (which was more like a box cupboard) "for a chat" one day. I was a bit apprehensive being called into the boss's office, but it turned out he wanted me to manage *La Costiera*. By this time, I had a young family, and needed an increase in my wages. We were getting tips at this stage of up to £120-£150 per week, which was good money then, but the actual wages weren't great. He agreed to increase my wages. Then I mentioned that my last train to the suburbs where I lived was at some stupid time like 11pm and I would have to depend on taxis to get home.

At that time, he owned a school of motoring on Alexandria Parade in the east end of the city. So, he drove me out there and showed me a fleet of six dual control Fiat 128s with L-plates he had parked at the driving school and said to me: 'Which one would you like?' I chose a red one and had it for four years.

The bar turned into a great success and Mr. Crolla promised us a magnum of champagne if we could make

£1,000 on a Friday alone. We did that over the Glasgow Fair Friday holiday, and he kept his word and brought down a large bottle of Dom Perignon. We really appreciated that. Within a few weeks we were turning over £3000 and sometimes more than that at weekends. I was only in my late 20s and felt I was doing well in the trade.

My father-in-law noticed my developing skills and he suggested that I manage a little pub he'd opened on Hope Street, one of the main streets in the city-centre. Previously It had been an "old man's pub" and he transformed it into a bar specialising in whiskies and called it the *Pot Still*. It was quite upmarket, and no-one was allowed in wearing jeans. It's still one of Glasgow's most famous pubs and renowned for its huge range of whiskies, though the ban on wearing jeans was lifted long ago. I had to learn a lot about whisky and drank a lot of it as well!

On Sundays we offered a "Scottish experience" aimed at American tourists. Along with the whisky we served traditional Scottish fare such as haggis, neeps, and tatties with black pudding along with stews. My number two in the bar, a nice, big, bearded guy called Sandy Martin from the Highlands with long hair (but then everyone wore long hair in the late 70s) wore a kilt – as we all did – and played the bagpipes. The Americans loved it and lapped it up.

My wife and I offered to rent the *Pot Still* but the owner, my father-in-law, refused. However, he did offer me the manager's post in a new venture he was opening. This was yet another part of the *Whitehall* complex which he turned into a wine bar, called the *Maltman*. This became one of Glasgow's first wine bars and Scotland's first non-smoking bar long before the nationwide smoking ban came in.

Clashes with the casuals

But I really wanted my own venture so, I leased a pub in Kilmarnock about twenty-files miles outside Glasgow. Unfortunately, it didn't work out too well. The main reason for that was because the pub had a lot of regulars who were also football casuals. This was now the early 1980s and football casuals – so-called fans who loved fighting with other fans – were a real problem for most football clubs. These guys were heavy and violent. Two guys in particular were always causing bother and, eventually, I had enough and said to both:

'The pubs for drinking in not fighting' and barred the two of them.

I realised after that I had to be careful; the place became even heavier for me. Finally, I thought to myself, I didn't need this hassle and gave the brewers who owned the pub two months' notice that I was quitting.

It was a Saturday at the end of July, a month before I was leaving, when a few coaches, full of people who'd been at an Orange Order parade turned up. Every single passenger that came off those coaches came into the pub – about 150 people in total. So, there we were, about four bar staff faced with this crowd, a few of whom were already the worse for drink. I phoned the police and they said: 'Well, there's not much we can do. You should have closed beforehand.'

I replied if I'd known this was going to happen, I would have 'closed the bloody pub!' They said they would send two cops in a van close by the pub to monitor the situation, but that was it; we were on our own. From about 6.30 till closing time, we had to put up with this lot and deal with them the best we could. It was a nightmare, but they gradually ran out of money which gave us a good, legitimate reason not to serve them anymore. But it was a slow process that lasted hours. Finally, we got them all out. The pub was a disaster area; those guys had wrecked the place, smashing up tables and chairs with broken glass everywhere.

As I was cleaning up and shutting the place, I noticed a car outside. Who was in it but the two guys I'd barred. Then the penny dropped. Why would the Orange Order target my pub? It was nothing to do with them. These two guys had brought those people from the Orange Order parade, knowing they would cause havoc, and we were outnumbered. It was the two guy's revenge. Their way of saying: 'We're the bosses, you're not!'

That was the final straw, and I handed the lease back immediately.

Into the nightclub scene

Licking my wounds from that experience I ventured into nightclubs and managed what was Scotland's first "super club", the *Metropolis* in the seaside town of Saltcoats on the Firth of Clyde. During that time, a friend's parents, who lived in Iran and were in poor health asked me to look after his club in Bathgate in West Lothian, which was called *Pzazz*, while he went back home to look after his parents. That was meant to be just for a few weeks but it lasted two years! However, I learned a lot about the nightclub scene which was invaluable for my next venture when I teamed up with my new business partner, Donald MacLeod, and opened a club which was located down by the river Clyde which we named the *Cathouse*. This was the early 1990s. That club is still open under that name but is now in Union Street in the city-centre.

The *Cathouse* became very popular and the centre of a vibrant music scene. It was an ideal setting. There was no dress code, we were within walking distance of the city centre and not far from the big new music venues which had recently opened in Glasgow such as the SEC (Scottish Exhibition Centre). As a result, a lot of celebrities who were playing there would show up such as Marti Pellow, who was a local boy, and the lead singer of Wet Wet Wet, who were at the height of their fame then. Marti was a party animal all right.

The *Cathouse* broke lots of new bands and rapidly became a fixture on the music circuit. We booked an American band by the name of Pearl Jam in 1992. They were a midlevel US band at the time we booked them mostly playing the college circuit. However, virtually overnight, they broke through into the big time and started playing sold out stadium gigs. So, here they were scheduled to play this small Glasgow club for £150 when they were now one of the biggest touring bands in the world!

Of course, their manager, not surprisingly, wanted to cancel the gig. But we stuck to our guns and held them to their contracts with the understanding that we would pay for a hotel for them. The gig was a sellout and a great success. By the way we also did the catering for them. They wanted what was then, for Glasgow, exotic Tex-Mex food such as guacamole, nachos, and the like. My wife, Josephine, who's an excellent cook, stepped up to the plate and they were delighted with what she served them.

Prince and the Garage gig

I was on a roll with the nightclubs in the mid-1990s. Glasgow was emerging as a thriving and lively nighttime economy. My next venture was one of the most successful. This was the *Garage* up on Sauchiehall Street right at the heart of Glasgow's nightlife district.

My partner and I, Donald MacLeod, were doing very well. Then a remarkable event occurred which is remembered as the most famous night in the *Garage's* history, and one of the most amazing in Glasgow's nightlife. Remember Wet Wet Wet? Well, their former tour manager had become a friend of mine. And his friend, believe it or not, was the then current tour manager for Prince, one of the biggest stars on the planet at that stage. On the night Prince was performing at the big Glasgow concert venue, the SEC, this guy, his tour manager, walks into the Garage and approached Donald and me and said Prince was wanting to do a small after-gig show after his appearance at the SEC. Could he play the Garage? I said: 'We can't afford to pay Prince, we're a wee Glasgow venue, on a different level from where he normally plays.'

There and then the tour manager offered us £15,000 in cash to put on the gig. We accepted, of course we did. There was one condition; there was to be no advance announcement. It would all be done by word of mouth. Anyone else who tried that we'd have said: 'take a hike!' but we knew once the rumour mill got into gear, we'd have a full house.

We didn't own the building. The man that owned it was the father of a popular local DJ on Radio Clyde called George Bowie. I called him; like me he was astonished, got in touch with his dad and we obtained the owner's consent.

Next thing, Prince's security guys appeared. Jeez, they were built like wardrobes, grunting with walkie-talkies and earphones which is now standard with security people at clubs but then looked like what you'd expect with the security detail around the President of the USA. We showed them around the place and between our people and his we devised a security plan and cover for the fire escapes and so on.

This was a midweek night in February 1995 and right at the end of the gig at the SEC, after the encore, I think it was Prince's drummer who announced the Man was going to do a "small gig" at the "Garaaage" with a long emphasis on the middle syllable. From that point on it was chaos; we were inundated. We charged £5 at the door, but knocked back more people than we let in, so we didn't actually make much money from it, but it was fantastic PR, and the night was brilliant. That's an evening I'll never forget.

Donald and I went on to open a few more clubs in the city: the *Shed* in the Southside and *Cube* back in the city-centre. *Cube* really did attract the celebrities as the *Cathouse* had earlier. We had football stars, TV people and so on. Eminem once rocked up after a show in Glasgow. Remember, at this time there was no social media, and we could spot paparazzi a mile away, so these people were guaranteed privacy in all our clubs. They could relax and chill out whereas now people would be trying to take a picture with them on their mobiles every minute.

Oasis, the flying bottle and the flying boat

But after Prince could we go any further? Well, yes, we could. After being discovered by Alan McGhee of Creation Records at *King Tuts* in Glasgow, we put Oasis on at the Garage and then we organised a two-day festival with them as the headliners at Loch Lomond. It has been widely recognised as one of their best performances and 55,000 people turned up each day. That was 1996, and later we organised for them to play at the SEC. However, that didn't turn out so well.

Not long after they'd started playing their set, some clown threw a plastic bottle at the stage, narrowly missing Noel Gallagher but striking the bass player on the leg. Noel was furious and he and the band stormed off the stage, never to return.

Before the gig I'd been approached by various PR people for top footballers to get them tickets both for the gig and access to the VIP area. We're talking then about Glasgow Celtic and Glasgow Rangers players like Paul Di Canio, Marco Negri and Paul Gascoigne, the legendary Gazza, who was then playing for Rangers. These were all regulars at our venues like the *Cube*.

We had these VIP guests, but the gig was abandoned. However, we managed to get them all backstage and meet the band. Then Gazza, who, incidentally, I'd bought a Harley Davidson moterbike from, invited us all back to his cottage on Loch Lomond side.

All of us: the football players, the band including the Gallagher brothers, Gazza himself and a retinue of security staff and bouncers headed back there. Once there, we all started playing football, but even though we've got topflight footballers with us, everyone's got a drink in them and it's just a kickabout. Gazza suddenly declared: 'you're all shite at football and yous canny play!' Then he announces we should go onto his powerboat which was tied up nearby.

This was about two in the morning and our judgement, shall we say, was impaired. We all clambered aboard, and Gazza started fumbling for the keys for the engine. Eventually he starts the engine. The only problem was no one had lifted the bloody anchor, so the boat powered up with a mighty roar and then bounced all over the water, almost tilting over. We were lucky it didn't capsize, and we emerged unscathed somehow. That cost two hundred thousand pounds or thereabouts of damage. All because some egit threw a plastic glass of water onto the stage!

Donald and I parted company, though we're still on good terms and I opened a series of venues including the *Butterfly and Pig*, a restaurant in the city which is still going strong and was the first gastropub in Scotland which my son redesigned and managed. I also started the *Buff Club* in the city centre. All these venues are still doing well despite the impact of COVID and cost of living crisis.

I bought the building that the *Butterfly and Pig* occupies and created the *Tearooms* downstairs serving afternoon tea and sandwiches which has proved very popular and endured over the years. The building also has space for our company offices.

I'm pleased to say that the cluster of venues I still own have weathered the storms of recent years.

Advice

Advice I'd give to people coming into this business? Firstly, times have changed dramatically both in Glasgow from what was a thriving bar, restaurant, café and club scene in the nineties and the noughties to where we are now where a lot of people in the trade are struggling.

Having said that, I started out with only £50. My wife said to me: 'You can do better with that £50 rather than putting it into a club.' I said to her: 'Wait and see.' That £50 set me up for what has been a good and successful career, but it takes hard work. If your intention is to make money in this game then you need to put the work in; it isn't going to come to you, certainly not by just sitting at home.

Any "secret" to my success would be that I've always enjoyed my work. It's never been a chore to me. If a problem arises my philosophy is: solve it, attack it, whatever you do don't shy away from it. As I keep saying to my managers, if you don't enjoy your work, then it's time to chuck it!

Michele's favourite dish: Puglia Beef Olive with a wee bit of lard.

Michele's favourite wine: I was brought up in a family that made our own wine, but if you're asking, I would say red Barolo wine.

7. GRAEME CHEEVERS & UNALOME: THE PATH TO FINE DINING IN GLASGOW

Graeme Cheevers is the chef patron of Unalome, a fine dining restaurant in the city which has been awarded a Michelin Star. How do you earn such an accolade? Graeme recalls the hard work, commitment and passion that led to it.

Beginnings

When I was about 12 or 13, I was dragged around our local golf courses by my father. I found golf boring and had no interest in it, so I ended up spending a lot of time in the clubhouse and would lend a hand making sandwiches and cakes for the golfers. That's where I started really enjoying cooking and fell in love with food.

At school I wasn't academic. I didn't enjoy studying unless it was hands on. I realised that I wanted to do something with my hands and cooking was ideal for that.

Soon, I'd outgrown the kitchen and wanted to expand my cooking horizons. Even though I was only 14 or 15 I didn't want to be at school anymore. Don't get the wrong impression of me, I wasn't an unruly or bad child in any way, it's just I felt school wasn't for me. Eventually, I came to an agreement with the school that I would leave at 15 and sit my Standard Grade exams at college.

A big motivating factor in this was that I was participating in a competition called Future Chef which I had started competing in at school and was allowed to finish at college where I managed to reach the regional finals.

During my time at college, I worked in a few restaurants in Glasgow, and I also applied to some of the top restaurants in the city such as the *Buttery* and *Etain*. But it was harder then than it is now to get a job in hospitality, especially as I was still only 15 or 16.

For a year-and-a-half I attended college five days a week and worked in restaurants in the evenings and at weekends. That was seven days a week getting up at 6 in the morning and often not finishing until 1am. They were long hours, but it gave me invaluable experience.

Breaking out

Once I'd sat my exams, I desperately wanted to leave college. It was boring, routine and I was sick of performing the same repetitive tasks week in, week out. To give you an example, on my hospitality course at college they would make us cook brown lamb stew every week. Without exaggeration, I would have that dish ready in half-an hour. The rest of the class would take three hours, to cook brown lamb and stew!

I'd be sitting there for the rest of the time bored witless, waiting for the others.

Finally, I left college and worked at the *Buttery* full-time for a few months. This was then probably Glasgow's most exclusive restaurant, and the Executive Head Chef was a guy called Willie Deans who went on to open his own restaurant in Perth. I was going to join him there, but at the last minute, I decided it wasn't for me and moved over instead to another of Glasgow best restaurants, *Etain*, where Geoffery Smeddle was head chef. I stayed there for a few years with Geoffery who became a good friend. Eventually, Geoffery opened his own place, a popular venue in Fife called the *Peat Inn*.

After a stint at *Etain* I left and moved across to New York for a while where I learned some new techniques.

When I came back to Scotland, I'd been working in restaurants for a couple of years, and I decided it was time to get acquainted with a wider spectrum of the hospitality industry, so I spent some time working in wedding and events catering. Basically, I was trying to find out for myself what it was I wanted to do and what I was particularly good at.

The catering trade is tough with long hours, poor wages, and often stressful conditions. If I wanted to make some money, I reckoned I would have to go into the more exclusive, upmarket area of fine dining where cooking and presenting food is far more artistic. Of course, the goal is to earn a Michelin Star. That was the motivation that was getting me out of bed in the mornings and putting in the hours. But getting into that level is not easy.

I knocked on a lot of doors and got some work experience, but often when I tried to get a permanent position or a higher grade, they would say to me bluntly: 'you're not good enough to work here.' You have to take that kind of comment on the chin. You need a thick skin to survive in this industry.

Serving fine dining on the bonnie banks

Eventually, I managed to get a position as commis chef under another famous executive chef, Martin Wishart, at the five-star *Cameron House Hotel* on the shores of Loch Lomond. I really thrived there. It was a great kitchen, a good environment working with a fantastic bunch of professionals and the customers were great. We opened only for dinner on weekdays and lunch and dinner at weekends. That gave us the time to focus on cooking and serving great-quality cuisine. Within a year, I was appointed head chef at *Martin Wishart, Loch Lomond* and awarded my Michelin Star.

Martin gave me a lot of independence and freedom at the restaurant; at times I was effectively running my own kitchen. There was such a variety of food, a fantastic mix and match, that gave me the preparation and confidence to consider running my own restaurant.

Then came the dreadful fire at *Cameron House* just before Christmas of 2017 and the hotel shut for a good while. That gave me a period to reflect what I wanted to do next and whether I should open on my own. But that was a massive step to consider.

I finally decided, I wasn't ready for that just yet. I would see if I could take on one more position under someone else's management that would give me that last bit of confidence and experience to go out on my own.

In 2018 I took up a position with a large five-star hotel in Oban that was bigger and busier than anything I'd done before. I thought it would be a good platform to work for another Michelin Star which I was awarded after eight months at the hotel. I stayed a further six months after that through a difficult period with low staff numbers, compounded by the fact the hotel was in such a remote location.

I'd managed to build up a good team as we went into the winter of 2019 when the bosses announced they were going to lay off half the kitchen and waitering staff as it was low season. I objected strongly, arguing you can't build up a strong team if you're going to break them up halfway through the year. That fell on deaf ears, and I left.

Going out on my own

This was months before the pandemic struck. I was briefly unemployed and carried out some consultancy work which came in handy. For a while, though, I had my eye on a restaurant tucked away in the west-end of Glasgow. It had previously been called the *Sisters* and had been run by a friend of mine, Jackie O' Donnell. I finally decided this was the opportunity I'd been looking for, so I bought it over and renamed it *Unalome*.

But this was during the pandemic and lockdown. There was no income coming in, but, equally, there were few outgoings either. In addition, lockdown didn't prohibit trades people from working, so, I used the time constructively to refurbish the place by working with a team of designers alongside my business partner. We stripped the building, rewired, replumbed and redecorated and built an open kitchen.

When we finally opened in June 2021, we were the second restaurant in Glasgow to have a chef with a Michelin Star which is, to say the least, a good quality mark. Although I had already been awarded two, I was very keen to have one for this new restaurant that I owned myself. The key to that was the food. I knew if I got things right on the plate it would get me what I wanted, i.e., the Star.

It has become a lot harder to earn a Michelin Star. The days when it was obvious who those besuited gentlemen with the glasses asking probing questions about the food were, have gone. Now it's much younger people coming into your restaurant who can be doing the assessing. But I'd been through the process before, so I knew what the pedigree they were looking for was. The bottom line is: if you're putting consistently good food on the plate, you're going to get it.

It took only eight months for *Unalome*.to be awarded a Michelin Star. That's fantastic, but the hardest part is keeping it. You've reached that level, and the world knows it. Now you've got to maintain those standards. Losing it would be a nightmare, but I've no intentions of letting that happen. But I don't want to sound churlish, getting a Michelin Star for my own place is a great feeling.

The restaurant has 50 covers with 22 staff, which is a lot for a small restaurant, but I think the quality of food and the customers deserve that input.

I try to maintain a balance between being in the kitchen and coming out to meet and speak to customers. People often want to speak to you to ask questions about the food and its important you do. But you also must make sure you're keeping standards high in the kitchen. Everything depends on the quality of the food.

Unalome has been a great success and I want to build on that and keep the staff and customers happy. I've got a great team around me including seven superb chefs. We're working with Glasgow Clyde College on a programme to train young chefs which I'm really excited about as that provides a solid basis for the future as some of them will go on to open their own places.

Our customers are great. We've very few complaints, though we do take all complaints very seriously.

I do laugh, though, when I see the odd customer walking out with the soap dispensers from the toilets sticking out of their tops, it means they must like the styling.

Advice

Start in the kitchen, work hard, don't complain about the long hours and low wages, be a sponge and learn as much as you can. Experience as many high-end restaurants as you can get into for a couple of years but don't stick around the one place too long. Build your confidence up and you'll know when the time is right to open your own place. Good luck.

Graeme's favourite dish: When you're cooking high-quality shellfish and meat all day, you really do want something different when you dine out, so I prefer Chinese or Indian food. I still love fish and chips.

Graeme's favourite wine: Barolo

8. RYAN JAMES AND THE BUTTERY: REVITALISING A GEM IN THE CITY

One of Glasgow's oldest fine dining establishments, the Buttery has been rejuvenated by award winning chef Ryan James. Ryan outlines the background to his success.

Beginnings
Back in the 1990s, my desire was to be an actor in the theatre and then on film and TV. I trained at the Royal Scottish Academy of Music and Drama where I graduated with a degree in Drama Studies. My Plan A was to be a Hollywood star. But the work was, to say the least, sporadic. Catering and hospitality became plan B.

To pay the bills, I started working in one of Glasgow's landmark restaurants, the *Rogano* in the city-centre whose interior was modelled on the Queen Mary, a liner built on the Clyde in the 1930s. It's been closed for several years now since covid and lockdown, but it was an iconic place, a real Glasgow dining institution.

I worked there for a few years, trained and mentored by Gordon Yuill who was the manager. Starting as a waiter and bar tender in the main restaurant. Gordon offered me my first management position in *Cafe Rogano*, which was in the basement. Throughout my time in *Rogano* I learned so much of what I still rely on today and formed my ethos of what makes a good restaurant great. It was also at that time my ambitions for the theatre took a back seat.

The *Rogano* was owned by Alloa Brewery, a big Scottish outfit who had several pubs and restaurants in the city. As my career progressed, I left *Rogano* to manage other venues for Alloa. It was at one of the places I managed for them, a pub/restaurant called the *Victoria and Albert*, in Glasgow city-centre, that I won their Manager of the Year award. That was a huge career boost.

Going upmarket with the ladies

After being around a few of their venues, I left Alloa Brewery to take the plunge into business with a partner to open a restaurant on the outskirts of Glasgow called *Gavins Mill*. That lasted three or four years and I gained a lot of experience from running that venture. We sold up after a good run and I decided that I was now ready to strike out on my own.

In 2002, I bought over a place in the West End of the city called *Two Fat Ladies*. The name had been coined by the original owner in 1989. It opened then with great critical success and as it coincided with my start at *Rogano* I knew it well. The name derived from its address: 88 Dumbarton Road and the bingo call: "88 - Two fat ladies."

Two Fat Ladies was a small, cosy, single-shop restaurant with 26 covers and was very popular. Its success stimulated me to open a city-centre unit in 2005 with the same name on the site of a former pub. From the outside the new venue also looked small, but it was in fact double the size of the West End site with 40 covers. Both sites did very well.

The *Buttery*

But the big prize for me was acquiring the *Buttery* which had a long and distinguished history. It was originally a pub called the *Shandon Bells* located at the bottom of a building which in the past had been part of a long row of tenements with a range of shops on the ground floor. These stretched in a long row all the way up to Argyle Street, which is still one of Glasgow's main shopping streets.

The area, known as Anderston, had been a densely populated district but, progressively, the population was decanted to make way for a new housing development, and the M8 motorway that was carved through the city. Without exaggeration, Anderston was bulldozed until the only two original buildings left standing were the *Shandon Bells* and a savings bank.

During the 1970s, 1980s and right up to the 1990s it was not uncommon across Glasgow to see entire streets which were deserted because all the tenements had been abolished, but the corner pubs which had served the people in those tenements were still standing, open and doing business even after the buildings above them had gone. The *Shandon Bells* was one of those though the building above it was still intact.

In 1967 the *Shandon Bells* became a restaurant called the *Shandon Buttery* and was revamped as a bar-come-restaurant. With a few gaps, it's been open since and is probably Glasgow's oldest restaurant of its kind. It was bought over by a prominent Glasgow restaurateur-come nightclub owner called Ken McCulloch in 1983 in association with Alloa Brewery. He and the brewery dropped the *Shandon* bit and renamed it simply the *Buttery* and transformed it into an upmarket restaurant.

Before I bought it, I'd had two previous experiences with the *Buttery*. The first was in 1990 when I went there as a customer. I could not believe the price of the food; it cost a fortune! I certainly couldn't afford to dine there on a regular basis.

The second time was when I was working for Alloa Breweries, who'd bought it over, and I was sent there for a brief period to act as a relief manager for about three weeks. Once again, I was astounded at the size of the bills people were paying. We're talking about hundreds of pounds in the 1990s for a three-course dinner. People were buying bottles of wine for £120 a skull. Today folk would struggle to pay that. But it was constantly busy and had quickly won a reputation for exclusivity. A lot of those bills though were being paid on expenses and with credit cards; it was very much what we would call an "expenses restaurant" in those days.

Eventually, in the early 2000s, Alloa Breweries sold it to a guy called Ian Fleming (no relation to the spy writer and Bond author) who operated it for a while. Then, catastrophe struck. Just before Christmas in 2006, there was a devastating fire. To make matters worse, Mr Fleming's own insurers wouldn't pay out for the damage. They claimed that there'd been something faulty with a vital piece of equipment which hadn't been maintained properly, or at least they couldn't find any records of it being maintained.

Fortunately, the insurers for the owners of the building paid out for a new roof, so the building was at least watertight and structurally intact. But it lay empty for a few months. Buoyed by the success of *Two Fat Ladies* I decided it was perfect as our next project.

Refurbishing and Reopening

I was aware that the restaurant trade was changing, and that people were eating out in different ways and in different places. The days of the expenses-based dining that had sustained the *Buttery* and other restaurants in the city were gone. But I firmly believed there was a new opportunity in reopening it and I was determined to buy the property. This was a huge gamble and if it went pear-shaped, I wanted some insurance by owning the property and be able to salvage something by letting it out or developing it.

I agreed a price with the property owner of the building and bought out the lease from Ian Fleming. To do that I had to get a loan from the bank. They were very supportive, and I secured the loan.

The refurbishment was meant to last three months; it took six. The cost was meant to be a certain amount; it was double that. Thankfully, the bank was still on board with me, but it was hairy. It wasn't just the financing or the refurbishment; the size of the premises was bigger than any I'd taken on before. Sure, I'd worked in bigger premises with Alloa Breweries such as the *Rogano,* but I was the manager, not the owner. It's a different level; you're het for everything.

I was going from 26 covers at Two Fat Ladies in the West End, to 40 in the city-centre site and was now nearly doubling that to over 70 at the *Buttery* with around 30 staff, including a kitchen staff of 12. But we got there, late and overbudget though it was and finally reopened in September 2007. I was petrified, given the prior reputation of the *Buttery* that I would be unable to match people's expectations and was about to fall on my sword or at least trip over my pride.

The Review

When we reopened there was still some scaffolding and building works outside and a few snagging issues inside. A few days before we officially opened, but were in the midst of a limited "soft" opening period, who walks in but the restaurant reviewer for the *Herald* (Glasgow's daily broadsheet newspaper), Ron McKenna, who as per his normal practice hadn't booked – he never did. With some trepidation we served him and his party and waited nervously for his review which would be in the following Saturday's edition of the *Herald*.

It was a stinker. He shot us to pieces. He wrote that his shoes were covered in cement because of the building works that were still outside. One line summed up the tone of the review: "These guys (our staff), normally self-assured, were like the crew on the deck of the Titanic heading forlornly for the iceberg while shouting 'help, help, help!'" Well, I thought, game over. I'd just spent a million pounds on this place, and courtesy of that review, we're dead in the water.

But it had the opposite effect. As a result of McKenna's bad review, everybody was talking about us and knew the *Buttery* had reopened. The phone never stopped ringing and bookings soared. And he had made some valid points which we immediately rectified.

We've never looked back since and we've grown by ten per cent annually, except of course for the covid years.

Like every restaurant owner covid and lockdown were a terrifying prospect. I was only a couple of months away from paying back the bank loan. It broke my heart to lock the doors and say adieu to all the staff who like me didn't know how we would financially survive. However, once the Government's furlough scheme kicked in we were able to retain our staff, and we knew we would survive. So long as the building was secured and watertight, once we'd put the lights out and locked the door, there were no more bills to pay or running costs to meet in the absence of any income.

Reflections on success

There's no simple answer to the question, why has the *Buttery* been so successful? One factor, I'm sure, is that we serve interesting but traditional food. I look to the past with our menus not the future. We've moved away from the era when the *Buttery* lived by customers paying on expenses. It's now a celebration restaurant and to reflect that the menu must suit the entire family. There has to be something for granny, something for the kids as well as catering for the more adventurous, gourmet-oriented palates. The other important factor that maintains our success is our people. They create the welcome and warmth that makes the *Buttery* a memorable experience and I'm so proud of them all.

There's a tendency now, not only in Glasgow but across the country, to go for new trends. People in the trade travel abroad, see something and think: 'Let's try that back home.' They open a few new places serving the latest trend and then there's a rash of people copying them. But the shelf life of these trends is always limited, and I think you're far more secure sticking to what's popular as what people like as fads and tastes can change quickly.

Small plates are the exception. I really thought that the trend for that type of dining would be short-lived, but it has lasted considerably longer and new small plates diners are opening all the time. But it's a very expensive way to eat out as well as being very labour intensive.

Don't dismiss Trip Advisor

In 2009 I found Google Analytics and for the first time found a report on our website and booking portal and noticed something interesting. Ninety per cent of traffic to the website was driven by Trip Advisor. That has been a gamechanger for the hospitality industry. Sure, you can approach people to put a review in for you on Trip Advisor, but you can't control what they're going to say about you.

There will always be some people, for whatever reason, who don't like you or your venue no matter what you do. That's life. I'm always suspicious of places that never get a bad review; that's just unreal. If you're operating well and serving decent food with efficient service those bad reviews will be massively outnumbered by the good ones

Lots of restaurateurs are nervous of or don't appreciate Trip Advisor, but it's just like looking in the mirror and not liking what you see. You can ignore it, or you can act on it. Remember, you haven't paid these people to write these reviews. In many ways, those reviews are worth so much more as they bring problems and oversights to your attention which a sycophantic paid review might gloss over or ignore. Most importantly, it helps you not to get caught up in your own bullshit and that's vital for keeping your feet on the ground. I really believe most people on Trip Advisor are sincere and are just writing about what they've experienced. I would strongly advise regarding Trip Advisor as a critical friend.

I'm proud of what I've achieved with the *Buttery* and the other ventures I've been involved with. They've become part of Glasgow's texture; part of its history and I can't say anything better than that.

Advice
Work from the ground-up. Once you've worked in the kitchens, go into management, and see how things work, how they're organised, how the different parts fit together. That way you'll find your strengths and weaknesses.

It's appropriate that I wanted to be an actor and ended up in the dining trade. In the servery at *Rogano* was a sticker on the inside of the doors "Smile You Are Going On Stage." That sums it up: you're on stage endlessly.

You need to be prepared for the hours you'll work and the stress and strains behind the scenes will sometimes be overwhelming. I thought I knew what stress was until I opened the *Buttery*, but that's the price you pay for a busy and successful venture. It's a jack-of all-trade, master-of-none type profession where you must keep a lot of balls juggling at the same time.

Above all, you need your wits about you, and you need to have genuine emotional intelligence with both customers and staff. I really don't believe you can do this job without emotional intelligence.

And if that hasn't put you off, the rewards are incredible and the satisfaction immense. This is a vocation. There's nothing else quite like it in the world.

Ryan's favourite dish: Scallops and langoustines. We are blessed to have the finest seafood in Scotland on our doorstep.

Ryan's favourite wine: Chateauneuf-du-pape.

9. SEUMAS MACINNES AND CAFÉ GANDOLFI: A JEWEL AT THE HEART OF THE MERCHANT CITY

For over 40 years Café Gandolfi has been a vibrant restaurant serving great food in Glasgow's bustling Merchant City. One man has been in charge all that time. Here Seumas MacInnes tells his story.

Beginnings

My mother and grandmother were *fantastic* cooks as were all my aunts; they were all intuitive Hebridean cooks. They lived next to an older couple who had no children of their own and they loved to borrow us from time to time. They would take me for lunch to all these incredible old romantic

Glasgow venues such as *La Fourchette, 101, Ferrari, the Malmaison* and the *St Enoch Hotel*.

The *St Enoch* was situated at the front of the old railway station in a stunning building that was a Glasgow landmark. They had an underground car park with valet parking. You could drive up to the entrance, as Uncle George (as we called him) did in his old Rover, and the valet would drive the car into the bowels of the hotel. After you'd dined sumptuously the valet would drive your car back to the entrance for you to collect and drive home. For me this was a little piece of Hollywood in Glasgow.

My father wanted me to be a lawyer, or an accountant – a 'professional' as he regarded such occupations, and regardless of whether that was ever a possibility, neither held any appeal for me. After dining in all those fabulous places, I wanted to be part of that scene. I went on to study hotel management. When I graduated, I thought I could immediately begin working in a good position in one of those beautiful restaurants, but, of course, it doesn't work like that. After college I ended up working for an industrial catering company where I lasted a year. The less said about it the better, suffice to say I never, ever want to work for an industrial catering company ever again!

After that, I opened a small catering company which I intended to be a personalised enterprise. I wanted to do grand and exquisite things such as choosing the flowers and selecting the appropriate wine and the crystal to go with people's choice of cuisine which would be delivered to them. But in the late 1970s not many people in Glasgow had that kind of cash. My culinary enterprise didn't last long.

Gandolfi beckons.

I needed a part-time job urgently. My sister's boyfriend worked in a place called *Café Gandolfi* which was earning a name for itself as a popular and reputable eatery in the Merchant City part of Glasgow. *Café Gandolfi's* arrival in the area under the stewardship of the then owner, Iain McKenzie began the transformation of this hitherto rundown district into a thriving destination in Glasgow.

My sister's boyfriend advised me to apply for a job there; at least it would pay the rent. I applied thinking I could become a chef, possibly a middle manager, even a head waiter. No such lofty positions were available and I was offered a job as a Kitchen Porter, a KP, the bottom of the ladder. But it was a start.

That was 1983 and I've been here since and I'm now the owner. How did I get here? For a start the kitchen at *Gandolfi* is quite small, you can learn a lot if you don't confine yourself to washing dishes. You get stuck in and make yourself useful and noticeable. The same is true today. I got to know that kitchen, the customer base of the Café, its house style, and its culture using my eyes and ears and watching all around me carefully. That experience was invaluable. And I learned so much.

For instance, I understand and can justify why the menu changes often. We do get people coming up to us saying: 'Why don't you have this or that on the menu? You always used to have that.' My answer to that is when I first started in the Café in 1983, we were making and serving cheese and mayonnaise baguettes – quite novel at the time. We innovate, progress and move on.

I worked my way up from KP to becoming a manager and latterly becoming Iain's junior partner. Eventually, Iain was keen to sell, and with the help of my wife, I was able to buy him out. That was nearly thirty years ago. I can't believe it's been that length of time. *Café Gandolfi* has been in the one location and is one of the longest continuous operators on the Glasgow dining scene which, otherwise, has witnessed so many changes. I've been here for more than forty years now and I remember finishing a shift once, sitting at a table and thinking: 'Here I am managing and owning a restaurant like this.' This is exactly where I wanted to be when I was young.

Keeping the Ethos and dealing with customers

I've gently developed an ethos which began with Ian McKenzie. Iain was visionary and showed me how to buy the best produce and to treat its inclusion in menus with the utmost respect. Even in the hardest of times, of which there have been a fair view of late, I have never demurred from that ethos.

My parents were from the island of Barra in the Outer Hebrides, and I wanted to bring some of that tradition to the restaurant. I was looking for a new slogan to sit alongside what was, essentially, an Italian restaurant. (Iain was a photographer and called the restaurant after a camera made by two Italian brothers called Gandolfi.) I consulted my mother, the Gaelic traditional singer Flora MacNeil. She came up with what has been my strapline and was a saying she'd often heard as a child: "*Deagh bhiadh, deagh bheannachd.*" It translates as "Well fed, well blessed." I thought that said it all.

We seem to attract lovely customers. Only very rarely has anyone given us any grief. One incident does stand out. A Chinese lady ordered finnan haddock which is poached haddock with poached egg and mashed potatoes. It's quite a salty dish as the smoking process is quite intense. The lady took a mouthful and started screaming, I mean at the top of her voice shouting: 'you're trying to poison me, it's so salty, its unbearable!' I rushed over to her and explained it was a poached fish but the smoking process unique to the part of Northeast Scotland from whence it comes, makes it quite salty. It's a bit like going into a Japanese restaurant, ordering sushi, and complaining it was raw! It is what it is, but she wouldn't stop shouting and was really angry.

There were these three ladies sitting close by to her. One of them rose from her table, came up to me and said: 'Seamus, the three of us are university educated but we come from the schemes (referring to the Glasgow housing estates). We'll have her if she doesn't stop shouting!'

Finally, the Chinese lady left, and I do assure you that I didn't encourage the Glasgow ladies to go for her. However, the inimitable Glasgow humour salvaged the situation.

And talking of Glasgow humour. My brother, Donald, also worked for me for a short period. He was, one day, serving a mother and her daughter and they wanted some cheese. My brother overheard the mother asking her daughter what Brie was. The reply: 'It's a bit like Dairylee with skin on.' She chose it and then asked Donald for a coffee requesting a 'Cappuccino without too much Chino…!'

Consistency and keeping standards

We have had 40 plus years of happiness despite recessions and a pandemic. Our customers have been overwhelmingly great. Another blessing has been having consistent, long-serving, loyal staff in an industry blighted by high staff turnover. That and an emphasis on quality, locally sourced food entices customers to come back and become regulars. Our customers also have lots of memories with us such as, to give a few examples, their parents having their first date, or a woman telling me her husband proposed here, a lady who brought her first baby here and so on. These are cherished memories for people which will, hopefully, last forever and so they should.

I think some of us proprietors or owners or whatever you want to call us fall into three categories. Some of us are restaurateurs, some of us are entrepreneurs and some of us are businessmen. I'm in the first category. My priorities are the food, the staff, and the customers.

When I first bought Iain out, I went back to the kitchen and spent a lot of time there. A good thing to have done in those early days as I wanted to be able to fill any breaches and convey to everyone that I understood their pressures. Steadily, however, I have allowed the kitchen staff to do what they know best and better than I know and I've concentrated on the role of front-of-house.

People can come into your restaurant heartbroken because, for instance, they've lost a parent or loved one and they're not wanting a conversation with you. Part of your job is to be aware of that; you don't know what people are living with.

That's why I firmly believe that not everyone can serve tables. I remember going to New York and expecting to be blown away by the service, as everyone assured me, I would be. Ok, the service was fast and efficient, but it was impersonal. I thought I had a twenty-dollar bill on my forehead as that was all they appeared to be interested in; not how I enjoyed my Ceasar Salad.

When famous people come to the Café, which is quite frequently, I like to think that *Gandolfi* is a safe place where they are treated with respect and allowed to enjoy their food and experience in peace. Most don't want a lot of fuss.

You do need to run a good ship, but I don't believe that cracking the whip and shouting and screaming at people is the most effective way of doing it. My approach is, better to show by example or sensitively explaining what the best way to do something is. It's a balance but you can't let things slip.

Advice

Would I encourage others to open a restaurant? Yes, but with a big qualification. The essential premium is that people need to have experience in the trade, be that waitering or managing. Coming in fresh is a recipe (no pun intended) for disaster. You need a good business plan and know exactly, based on prior experience, what you want to produce. I don't know how many times I've heard people with no history or knowledge of the trade come up with romantic ideas about opening a café or a diner and my first reaction is a frankly incredulous: '*Are you sure?*'

Recently, one customer my age said to me: 'Seamus, I've got this great idea for opening a restaurant.' He told me what it was, and I asked him: 'What age are you." A bit reluctantly and hesitatingly, he said: 'Fifty.' I came back at him: 'You need loads of experience at the coalface in this game, and you'll only get that if you're in good shape and in your twenties and thirties because you'll work all the hours God sends.' And that about sums it up.

I'm no hypocrite when I say that because I've no intention of going on and on. I plan to take more time off and get more holidays. This is an all-consuming business that impacts on your family life. My wife has now retired, and she has plans to do things and go places and I want to do them with her before it's too late.

I definitely don't want to be that old guy sitting at the table in the corner with a glass of red wine watching the world go by and one of my children shouting: *'There's the taxi for Seumas!'*

Seumas's favourite dish: I was proud that *Café Gandolfi* was the first to serve Stornoway black pudding as a non-breakfast dish and put it on the map.

I also love, "deconstructed" Cullen Skink, which is lovely and elegant. I'm always very pleased when someone orders that.

And I could never take caramel shortcake off the menu. I thoroughly recommend it. *Café Gandolfi* was the first place to make it.

Seumas's favourite wine: Pinot Noir and Sancerre

10. PAUL STEVENSON: PAESANO PIZZA, THE MAN TAKING PIZZA TO NEW LEVELS

Glaswegians love pizza and Paul Stevenson with his Paesano Pizza outlets has brought a whole new dimension to that iconic Italian dish. Paul relates the background to his incredibly popular venture.

Beginnings

I started out in the rag trade, selling men's clothes. I opened my first shop, called *Bazaar*, in 1979. It was quite successful at first, but during the eighties the independent menswear business was coming to an end as the big designer labels were moving in and taking over. I saw the signs and sold up.

I'd always had an interest in food, so I set up a corporate catering company for businesses which I called *Hungry's Catering*. There's now quite a lot of these company's but then it was novel, at least in Glasgow, and ahead of its time. I employed about half-a-dozen girls who prepared the food under my instructions. We worked Monday-to-Friday office hours, nothing like the seven days and all hours which are standard for restaurants.

One time we had a contract to cook lunch at a boardroom meeting being held at one of Scotland's largest law firms. The meeting was to complete a deal worth millions of pounds. However, in the middle of cooking steaks, I set off the smoke alarm in the building! Everybody, including of course the people at the board meeting had to be evacuated and wait outside until the fire brigade came along and gave the all-clear.

Diversifying

Corporate catering was successful, but in 2002 I decided to diversify into the restaurant business and opened *The Italian Kitchen* in the Merchant City area of the city. I had intended to employ a head chef who came with fantastic recommendations. He started two days before we opened and I decided to check him out and asked him to cook me a couple of dishes – two steaks, one medium-rare, the other rare in a red wine sauce with chips. I thought this would just be a formality and no problem for this guy. He went downstairs to the kitchen to make a start on the dishes.

After twenty minutes, there was still no sign of him, so I went down to the kitchen to find him throwing burnt steaks into the bin! I thought, what have we got here? I can't trust this guy on his own in a busy kitchen in a new restaurant!

I ended up becoming the head chef myself which I'd never done before. I'd cooked of course before, but being a head chef and running a kitchen is on a different level. *The Italian Kitchen* opened on Saturday 21st December, three days before Christmas; the busiest time in our trade with the office parties and so on and I was put right in at the deep end. I did get some assistance from another chef, Vincent Brolly, but for three years, he and I were stuck in the kitchen. That was a baptism of fire and my hurried introduction to becoming a chef.

The Italian Kitchen became very popular, but soon a lot of similar restaurants opened around us. Competition became quite intense, our margins started slipping (we didn't do a reduced lunch sitting, our prices were the same throughout the day) and it was becoming increasingly difficult. I felt under incredible pressure with being a head chef and managing a busy restaurant. My health suffered so, I decided to quit when I was still ahead and sold the restaurant in 2015.

An oven adventure

Around this time a pizzeria called *Franco Manco* had just opened in Brixton in London. I paid a visit and was quite impressed by the operation and the concept and decided I would open a similar venture but add my own spin and style to it.

I found this place on Miller Street, right in the heart of the city-centre, near all the main shopping streets, car parks, bus routes, train stations and so on. As soon as I walked into it, I loved the size and shape of the place and decided this was the ideal location for my new pizzeria in Glasgow – *Paesano*.

We brought over a huge pizza oven from Italy weighing three-and-a-half tonnes. But it turned out the floor in the premises couldn't take that weight. I had to bring in this specialist logistics company, and they came up with a solution. First, they took away the shopfront, windows, and doors because the oven was far too wide to get in. Then they put metal sheets under the massive oven and installed pads on the oven legs, before pumping compressed air which allowed the oven to float (no kidding that's what it seemed like) across the floor until it was securely installed and fitted at the back. It was an amazing job, even just to watch it. But that wasn't the end of it.

Keeping it simple

My idea for *Paesano* was to combine consistency with simplicity. The product had to be of consistently good quality; I'm obsessed with that. The focus was on one main product, pizza, done well. It was the simplicity of the offer that I concentrated on. A lot of Italian restaurants, I feel, have overly complicated menus which can confuse people and put them off. Ours is a simple menu. Most of the recipes are my own and I also take time to write simple descriptions on each item on the menu and what the ingredients are.

Simplicity and a focus on one product allow us to sell at reasonable and competitive prices which attracts a wide range of people from businesspeople to students. Since the day we opened back in 2015 we've been extremely busy.

To ensure consistency and good quality the chefs do tastings of every item on the menu daily. This is the best measure of quality control. And it works. Five-to-six thousand people come into the Millar Street *Paesano* alone weekly and since we've opened eight years ago, we've only had a handful of complaints. You can have the nicest surroundings and environment in the world, but if the food is of poor quality, it's no good. My motto to the chefs is simply: *If in doubt don't put it out!*

I've got a great management team who now run the business day-to-day, and an excellent group of chefs. I couldn't do without them.

Expansion to the West End

In 2017 I decided to open a second pizzeria in the West End on Great Western Road an area as busy and as accessible as the city-centre venue. I checked out the building beforehand. The space, the layout and its location were ideal. We opened in April and were busy from the get-go.

During lockdown we didn't open for takeaways in the city-centre, but we did in the west-end, and had phenomenal business. The income from takeaways actually exceeded sit-in takings at the West End restaurant for quite a while. At one point during that period, I took a picture of people queuing along Great Western Road for takeaways.

I'm delighted that, post-lockdown, we're back up and running and business is booming at both restaurants. We've recently recorded the best takings we ever had. A few people have tried to copy what we've achieved, but none have so far succeeded, but we'll never be complacent.

I have had some bad health scares over the past few years and a total of three operations in about three years, so, now, I must take it a lot easier. But there's a great team in place and that allows me to take it easy and have a much more hands-off role, though I'm still obsessive about quality and alert to any downturns in standards. I feel, though, that I can confidently delegate to professionals who share my values when it comes to running a busy restaurant.

There are a total of 109 staff employed across the two restaurants and, inevitably, there's a turnover of waitering staff. Serving over ten thousand people a week is hectic; at busy times it's just nuts. It's not for everybody. Someone can start with us, work a demanding shift and we never see them again. To mitigate that I intend to put the staff on a four-day week to give them a better work/life balance.

Advice

Work on your instinct. A lot of people come into this trade without thinking it through. You've got to consider what the market is for what you propose to serve, what's the business model to sustain it, the shape and size of the premises you're going to operate from, how do you ensure good quality in terms of service and food. All of these are interlinked; fail on one and it impacts the rest. Don't just think "I'm going to open a restaurant". Think it through carefully. Regrettably, there are far more failures than successes in this game.

But if you do come up with a good concept and it succeeds, there's nothing more rewarding.

Paul's favourite dish: Spaghetti Vongole. My favourite non-pasta dish is roast chicken.

Paul's favourite wine: Barbaresco for a red wine and Gani for a white wine.

11. GILLIAN EAGLESON: SCOTLAND'S FIRST FEMALE EXECUTIVE HEAD CHEF IN A FIVE-STAR HOTEL

Starting out as a waitress, Gillian worked her way up to becoming first female Executive Head Chef at one of Scotland's leading five-star hotels. Gillien recaps her remarkable story.

Beginnings

I really fell into hospitality as I'd never thought of going into it when I was young. I went to university, but realised after six months this wasn't for me. When I left university, I needed to find a job. A family member alerted me to a job as a breakfast waiter at *La Bonne Auberge* which was located within the *Holiday Inn* in Glasgow city centre. I applied and got the job, even though it involved a very early start, and I wasn't a morning person at that stage. But it was a foretaste of things to come.

The hotel offered a job swap scheme where people could spend a day or two in different roles at the hotel. I was hanging about with the kitchen staff a lot, so I was keen to spend a day there. I loved the experience and got instant job satisfaction from seeing what you've made go out on a plate.

Every time there was a job going in the kitchen, I would apply but got knocked back as they were only taking on people with experience. It didn't help either that I was dating one of the chefs (who later became my husband) and they weren't sure how that would work out.

But the irony was that a lot of the people they took on only lasted a day or two. Eventually, after much persistence on my part, they caved in and let me work in the kitchen. My initial impressions weren't wrong. I really liked working in the kitchen and my experience at *La Bonne Auberge* gave me a good foundation in how a kitchen worked. In total I spent two years front of house and three years in the kitchen while there. I loved the cooking, the buzz, and the teamwork. I surprised myself as I'd never cooked at home, and I was encouraged at *La Bonne Auberge* to try things out for myself.

In the door and going Five-Star

I moved on from there to work in the five-star *Blythswood Hotel*. Before I started there, I had a terrible interview for that position. I was feeling really nervous, and they asked me all sorts of technical questions about various dishes. I just confessed I didn't know. I had a wealth of experience in the various food sections at *La Bonne Auberge* and knew how to make dishes, but I didn't know the reason or the science behind why this or that dish had to be a certain way or a certain temperature! However, they appreciated my honesty.

Some weeks later they wrote back to me saying they were fully staffed but they'd put me on a reserve list. Then, out of the blue, they phoned, asking if I'd be interested in a trial shift to see how I coped. Their hours were 8am to 11pm; that's right, 15 hours! But I couldn't knock back the chance and said, 'yes.' They asked me what day I'd be free. I was still working at *La Bonne Auberge* and was about to work ten days straight with two days off which was a Wednesday and Thursday. I said 'Thursday' which would have given me a day's break, but the guy from the *Blythswood* said 'could you not do the Wednesday, please?' I didn't want to risk the opportunity, so I said 'yes,' and ended up starting my trial shift at 8am after working for ten days!

I researched the menu before the trial shift and I'm so glad I did. There were items on that menu which are popular today, but less well-known then such as quinoa, quince paste, monkfish cheeks and so on, that I had never heard of. I looked up the ingredients and how best to prepare them, so much so, that I didn't appear too much out of my depth on the day of my trial shift.

If I thought the kitchen at *La Bonne Auberge* was busy the *Blythswood* was on a different scale. It was large and best described as organised chaos. I recall the executive chef at the time, Dan Hall, coming round just before dinner service was beginning and depositing a dozen Mars Bars on the counter in the kitchen and I thought 'that's my breakfast!' because I hadn't stopped since eight am.

I somehow survived that shift and was offered a position with them. It was a great experience as I worked my way through the different sections of the kitchen. Chefs are generally not regarded as the most intelligent of people which I think is grossly unfair. It's a very taxing, mentally challenging profession where you have to use a lot of time management skills and juggle a lot of balls in the air to make sure everything is coming together. My respect for chefs has been really heightened over the years I've worked in kitchens. It's a very skilled occupation and not everybody can do it.

A lot of the time I was asked to cover for the pastry chef and found I really enjoyed working in that section, but I was never allowed to work there full time. After six years at the Blythswood I started looking for another opportunity and was offered a place at a new venture called the *No I Chocolate Factory* where I was told I'd be trained in how to make chocolate. But it wasn't as billed, I never received the training, and I ended up mainly making kid's birthday cakes and preparing café food.

Working 5-Star: Afternoon teas & the quirks of celebrities

The *Blythswood* got back in touch and offered me a full-time position as a pastry cook working under their pastry chef. I went back, but the pastry chef had, unfortunately, left by this time. However, I knew the section well and I had control over what I wanted to put on the menus, so I was quite content to stay there for a few more years.

When people think of 5-star hotels they think of somewhere quite dignified, but the pace was incredible morning-thru-to-night. You need to be thick-skinned and resilient working in a high-pressure kitchen like that. You're on your feet constantly, spending up to 12-15 hours per day with the same people. Often, we'd be making 2-300 afternoon teas on a day.

Those afternoon teas were particularly popular, and I remember when this new sandwich chef began his first shift. We had 200 teas to serve that day and he said to me, with an incredulous look on his face:

'I've got to make four finger sandwiches per person, that's a total of 800 sandwiches?' And I came back at him with:

'Yep, and I've got 1,000 cakes to make and 400 scones!'

People also have this perception that fine dining is sedate, and you can spend two-and-a-half leisurely hours over your food, which is true for the customers, but behind the scenes in the kitchen it's frantic.

A lot of celebrities stayed at the *Blythswood,* but we had little to do with them. The only time we would have any dealings with them is when they brought their personal chefs with them, and we'd give their chefs an induction tour of the kitchen so they could get set up.

The people in the hotels who were in contact with celebrities were a section called Guest Relations who liaised with the team that was looking after them and dealing with all their demands. And, from what we heard back in the kitchen, they could be quite demanding. For example, there was the celeb who wanted a specific type of candle which had to have a specific scent and the candle also had to burn non-stop for 24 hours. Guest relations were all over Glasgow searching for that.

Sometimes, on Friday and Saturday nights, just before the hectic dinner servings, we'd often be plunged into darkness in the kitchen. It was a nightmare trying to plate up by candlelight or use small portable panini stoves to heat up huge pots. The reason for the power cuts at that time was reckoned to be the result of a sudden power surge brought on by hundreds of hairdryers being switched on at the same time just before dinner in most of the hotel rooms.

Going Executive

I didn't go to college to learn to cook. I learned on the job and from other people. I often made mistakes in the kitchen, but that's the way you learn. A lot of the time your also training staff on the job and that's a big responsibility. You need to survive on your wits and no two days are ever the same. Ok, all that sounds like a moan, but the rewards and the job satisfaction when you've got through a busy day and a couple of hundred people have enjoyed the food you've made is immense.

During my second stint at the *Blythswood* I started to learn more about the back of house functions at the hotel such as payroll, stock checking, rotas, and orders, but my first love was always in the kitchen, cooking.

In 2017 the hotel was expanding. At the same time the Executive Chef was leaving, and I was encouraged to apply for his position. I've always struggled with self-doubt mainly because I wasn't trained as a chef. Even though I was a hard worker, reliable and wasn't afraid to get my hands dirty, I just didn't have the confidence to take on an Executive Chef's position.

It was fortunate I didn't take up the post because the former Executive Chef had moved onto the luxury *Cameron House Hotel* on the shores of Loch Lomond, but stayed only a short time there before coming back to the *Blythswood* and took up his old position. Just as well I never took it!

Soon after though, he received an internal promotion to become Executive Head Chef at the *Grand Central* at Glasgow Central Station, which is owned by the same group that owns the *Blythswood*. I decided, ok now's the time to go for it, but they dragged it out for ages before they confirmed my position as Executive Head Chef, the first woman to achieve that role at a 5-Star hotel in Scotland and the first at the *Blythswood* as all my predecessors had been males.

It felt great to have achieved that position having started out as a breakfast waiter. It shows what's possible if you apply yourself and are prepared to work hard.

In 2020 the pandemic struck and there was a restructuring at the hotel. A whole chunk of middle management was being made redundant and all the remaining posts had to go through a competitive interview process. As it turned out my husband, who'd worked at the *Blythswood* for years (and had also been second head chef on the Royal Scotsman luxury train for a time), had been appointed the head chef covering both the *Blythswood* and the *Grand Central*. So, not only would I be up against my own husband for a competitive interview., which I didn't relish the prospect of one bit, but I realised it would be a huge job taking on overall charge of two extremely busy kitchens and I didn't want that level of responsibility.

My husband and I had spoken about starting a family and I thought now was the right time. I loved my job so much it took a global pandemic to make me leave it.

Starting a baking business

Apart from starting a family, I had to seriously think about what I was going to do. Cooking was my whole life. For a while I'd been contemplating starting my own baking business. I knew full well from my time at the *Blythswood* that afternoon teas were extremely popular, and I loved making them, so that was the market I focused on.

I advertised widely and got quite a lot of business during lockdown. I'd rock up at people's doors with my masks and a full contactless delivery service complete with roll-out table and boxes with the teas which the customers could lift from the table. It's been quite a success, and I can make up to 90 afternoon teas from my home kitchen.

I do a lot of celebration events such as birthdays with custom made cakes to order with all sorts of weird and wonderful decorations on them. Recently, for example, there was a mother who ordered a birthday cake for her son. She wanted it adorned with a very specific size and colour of a shark, with the shark depicted swallowing the boat which also had to be of a very specific size and colour. I was delighted when the mother sent me a video of a delighted child ecstatic at the cake I'd made.

I've got an edible printer at home, and I was able to make these biscuits for a customer with a picture of Lewis Capaldi on the top next to a replica miniature of a Buckfast bottle. She loved it.

I've never really encountered sexism in the business. As I say, it's a very high-pressured job, there will be choice words exchanged but you give as good as you get. But thankfully, I've never been the victim of sexism or harassment. I'm not saying for a second it doesn't occur. I was invited onto a radio programme to discuss this very topic with another female chef. She had a very different experience from me and had witnessed sexism in the kitchens and difficulties dealing with some male chefs. It does happen, but I've been fortunate in working with a great bunch of professional people, many of whom have become friends.

Advice
Have a good work ethic, use your wits about you and be able to get on with people. Own up to any mistakes you make; don't try to avoid responsibility. These are essential qualities for working in a kitchen. If you're not prepared to work hard, you'll be found out rapidly in a busy kitchen. I know of people who've started a shift and just disappeared. You'll hear them say: 'I'll just take the bins out,' and they're away, never to be seen again. Working in a kitchen can be daunting and you need to be prepared otherwise don't even consider it.

But if you stick it, the rewards are amazing. I can't say that too much. The buzz, the teamwork, the satisfaction you get, the ability to learn or make new recipes, to be creative is wonderful. If your new, be prepared for hard work but absorb and learn everything you can. You can go a long way in this business.

Gillian's favourite dish: When I go into a restaurant, I always check the menu to see if scallops and cheesecake are available. At home I love mince and tatties. Confession: When I was working in the kitchens, finishing at 11 and starting again at six, I could often be found with a pot noodle at home as you just didn't have the time or the energy to cook something.

Gillian's favourite wine: I prefer white: Sancerre or Gavi.

12. MARCO GIANNASI: REST & BE THANKFUL ON THE SOUTH SIDE OF GLASGOW, THE BATTLEFIELD REST

Marco is the successful proprietor of the Battlefield Rest restaurant in Glasgow's Southside. Here he recounts how he has transformed a dilapidated former tram shelter into a very popular Italian eatery which has become a landmark for diners not only in the Southside but also further afield.

He has also conserved an iconic building in the Battlefield area and, indeed, has made part of it an apiary which produces locally produced honey and helps preserve the local bee population.

Marco has recently turned his hand to writing short stories with a distinctive culinary theme.

Beginnings

I've been involved in the restaurant trade for over fifty years, and I've basically grown up in that kind of environment. As they say, it's in my DNA. One of my earliest, fondest memories is of my dad ordering wine from a company called Giordano who were based in London. At that time there were no wine distributors in Scotland and my father had to make a very specific bulk order of 90 cases of wine each month from London. As a six- or seven-year-old kid I used to lock myself into the wine cellar and spend a happy couple of hours putting the bottles on the shelves with the labels facing all the same way. For that I would be given a bonus treat of sweets for my labours as I was obviously too young to get some wine!

My father's first restaurant in Glasgow was *Canasta* in 1954 which he ran until it was demolished around 1968. Following this my parents opened *L'ariosto* in the city centre in 1972.

Sadly, my father passed away a year later, leaving the restaurant without a direction. This was a big challenge, so my mother and I drove all the way to Scotland from my hometown in Italy, Castelnuovo Di Garfagnana, to help the manager with the running of the place.

Soon afterwards, we renovated an old building in Balfron in Stirlingshire and turned it into a pub/restaurant. Then, in 1992, I came across this iconic landmark in Battlefield which was lying empty. It had been the first tram shelter to be built in the UK in 1914 and was intended to be a prototype for other tram shelters. However, as we know, the First World War broke out that year and no further shelters were built. So this is the only one of its kind and is quite unique.

Anyway, I was keen to purchase it and convert it into a restaurant, so I bought the building for **one pound** and transformed it into the successful venue it is today.

Know your customers.

When I was the landlord of the pub in Balfron I was one of the youngest publicans in Stirlingshire - only about 22 or 23. It was a rural setting, and all the regular customers were locals; everybody knew everybody else. I was told there was a tradition that, at the end of the night, if a customer's a little bit tipsy, you should make sure they're okay and maybe even take them home, if necessary.

One night, this regular, an old gentleman we'll call "Ben," was very tipsy. Taking on board that local tradition and striving to be a good community pub landlord, I put him in the back of my estate car with the intention of driving him home. He had a good drink in him, but he still managed to give me directions to his home (remember there was no Sat Nav then).

Eventually, he pointed me to a house and said he wanted a breath of fresh air. It was a lovely summer's night, and I very gently got him out of the car and escorted him to his front door. He said: 'Just leave me here,' which I did thinking I'd done him a good turn getting him home safely and I drove away.

Next morning, back in the pub, eight o'clock sharp, there's a furious banging on the door. I opened it to see this very angry and upset lady who started shouting at me; I'd no idea why. At length, she calmed down enough for me to understand why she was so annoyed with me. She was complaining that a very drunk man was left at her front door, and she managed to find out from him that I, your friendly local community publican, had driven him there! That was bad enough. But then it transpired that the lady in question was a prominent member of the local Free Church which is very anti-alcohol and strictly pro-temperance. Well done, Marco, that was good relationship building, indeed!

I learned a sharp lesson there. Assess the situation and get to know your customers well before diving in.

The Stained Trousers

L'ariosto, the popular Italian restaurant in Glasgow city centre I took over from my father, had a lot of booths where people could dine in privacy and with discretion. At lunchtime, we had a lot of custom from all the local offices such as solicitors and accountants who appreciated the privacy of the booths. There was a very different ethos around drinking at lunchtime back then and long liquid lunches were quite common. As a result, we got to know the companies and their staff very well.

One lunchtime, back in the 1990s, the head waiter approaches me to inform me that the secretary for the head of one of the local solicitors' offices has spilled a glass of red wine over her trousers. He, the head of the firm, is due back in the office for a very important meeting where the secretary will be taking notes, and this will be an awkward and embarrassing situation.

The place was really busy that lunchtime. I said to the head waiter: 'What do you want me to do?' Half-jokingly, I added: 'Tell her to take off her trousers and we'll clean them for her!' He went away and a couple of minutes later, to my astonishment, he reappeared with a pair of trousers with a noticeable red stain on them.

'What have you done?' I asked him. 'I was only joking.' But there was no going back, and I had to do something and think on my feet. The firm and its boss were good customers, they lunched there frequently, and they spent lavishly on food and drink. Suddenly, I had a flash of inspiration. Fortunately, just next door, there *was* a dry cleaner's shop. We took the trousers in, and the staff told us we'd have them ready in an hour. Back in the middle of a very busy restaurant at the height of lunchtime, we had the comical situation of a pretty young lady sitting at a table with her colleagues and her boss minus her trousers. I can assure you that, for the hour it took to get those trousers back to her, that lady had the most exclusive service ever. I don't think any other restaurant could offer the same service and attention as the young lady received that day.

The trousers came back in the hour cleaned, the stain gone, and they left for their meeting, happy and satisfied.

Yes, the customer is *always right* no matter what.

Saturday Night Walk-ins

There was another funny incident earlier at *L'ariosto* when I was learning the trade there. I was in my mid-20s, still quite new and depending on the rest of the staff to guide me. The year was 1978 and in those days in Glasgow city centre there was a strict dress code for customers dining in restaurants such as *L'ariosto*, especially at weekends: no jeans, trainers, T-shirts, or casual wear. Ties were compulsory as Saturday night was a dinner-dance affair. These rules were strictly enforced.

One Saturday night, quite late on, in walks a group of guys wearing leather jackets, waistcoats without jackets, denims and one of them had a bandana. They were chatting away to each other, and it was clear from their accents they weren't locals. There were about half-a-dozen of them. The restaurant manager approaches them and says: 'Sorry, gentlemen, but you have no ties, and we have a strict code.' They seemed to accept that, turned round, and left. But I noticed a lot of the other customers appeared to recognise them. Some people at a table said to me as I passed them:

'Do you know who those people you just refused entry to were?'

I said: 'no' and they told me they were the band, Black Sabbath, who were headlining at the famous Glasgow Apollo that night. I was astounded and thought how stupid: we've just refused a major international rock band. How would that affect our reputation? I told the manager, but he didn't know who they were and insisted rules and standards had to be maintained.

To my great surprise, about forty minutes later, I noticed from the back of the restaurant, the guys walking back in. But this time they were all wearing ties, even those with the wide-open shirts and bare chests. The manager was speechless as they went up to him. One of them said to him, I still recall, in an American accent:

'Well, you told us to come back with ties. And we've all got ties now. So, can we have a table for six people?'

The manager, of course, couldn't refuse. I helped to serve them and eventually plucked up the courage to ask:

'Where did you get the ties from? It's the weekend and everything's closed!' And the guy with the American accent said:

'Well, we went out onto the streets and stopped each guy we saw who was wearing a tie and offered them some money for their ties. We got six and that was enough to get us back in here.'

Now that's enterprising, I thought, and deserves some respect. I'm glad to say they enjoyed their meal.

Cooking Pasta by Candlelight at the Rest

During one very busy lunchtime before Christmas at the *Battlefield Rest,* we had a power cut. At first, we thought, ok, twenty minutes, half-an-hour and the power will be back on. But it didn't come back on. We were fully booked that lunchtime and the place was filling up rapidly.

The chefs were becoming agitated as there was no power for the ovens. So, I phoned Scottish Power to enquire what was happening, only to be told it was a major power failure and it would be at least half-a-day before the power would be restored!

We were looking at a disaster with a lot of customers who we didn't want to turn away, especially at that time of the year. But what were we going to do? Marino, our head chef, who's been with the restaurant right from the beginning, an old hand with a cool head, says to me that if he could have some candles and a couple of small camping stoves, he could rustle up some good food, even for about sixty hungry people. But where could we get the stoves from and in such a short time?

Then my wife, Yellena, came up with the idea of going on Facebook and making an emergency appeal for stoves. Immediately we got a notification back. A customer, who lives only a short distance away posted they had two little stoves. Do we want them?

I ran out and collected them, they were tiny wee things, and handed them to Marino. I asked him: what can you do with them? He shook his head and said: 'These are only wheat pans, so there's very little I can cook on them.'

'So, what can you do?' I asked him, exasperated. He replied drolly:

'Spaghetti or spaghetti and that's it.'

Well, as they say in English, needs must. So, I went out to the customers and said to them: 'We've got a power cut. It's out of our hands and it's probably going to last for a couple of hours. All we can offer is two types of spaghetti: meat or vegetable. And we can provide some bread, olives, and sliced meats to accompany.' Amazingly, or maybe unfortunately for Marino, they all decided to stay.

All during that lunchtime Marino laboured in the otherwise pitch-black kitchen with ten candles cooking up delicious pasta which we served to grateful customers. He worked a miracle that afternoon.

Halfway through, I took a picture of him in that kitchen cooking furiously by candlelight and posted it on Facebook. The *Glasgow Times* picked up on it and published the story next day in the paper. Customers were delighted as they'd never had the experience of a chef preparing dinner for them by candlelight. That earned us incredible publicity. That's what happens when you build a good relationship with your customers.

But, apart from the staff who worked incredibly hard that day, the two heroes of the story are Marino the chef who rose to the challenge so well and our neighbour who supplied those stoves.

Thanks to both of you.

Marino, Marco's loyal chef for many decades

Advice

I'd say to anyone wanting to come into this business, the prime ingredients are honesty, consistency, and hard work. Also, be upfront with your customers as, for example, the episode with the power cut at the *Battlefield Rest* and be straight with them.

Always remember your customers are your salesforce. If they like you, they will be your greatest publicist and marketing force. But, equally, if you're bad, particularly in terms of quality and consistency, then word gets around, especially nowadays with social media, and that can kill your trade very quickly.

At the *Rest* we have customers who have been coming for decades. We get to know them, and that personal touch is important. There is a customer who was first brought to the

Rest by his parents as a baby in his pram in 1994, who now comes to the restaurant with his own baby in a pram!

I've recently retired and taking a step back now, though I'm still involved with the business. The people who have taken over, Alex and Jane, are competent and know the business inside out (Alex worked at the *Rest* for many years). They'll apply those same principles of honesty, consistency, and hard work, to keep the *Battlefield Rest* as a thriving restaurant for the future.

Marco's favourite dish: Polenta with rabbit and olive stew. Brings back fond memories of my nonna.

Marco's favourite wine: Morellino Di Slansano. A terrific Tuscany red.

13. JEN DOHERTY & ALEX MATHESON: IN WITH THE NEW AT THE BATTLEFIELD REST

Taking over a successful restaurant is always a challenge. Husband and wife, Jen and Alex explain what inspired them to take over the immensely popular Battlefield Rest and their first year in charge.

Beginnings

Jen: I've always been attracted to hospitality. This goes back to when I was young and my grandparents' owned pubs. This meant that I was familiar and comfortable with being around hospitality settings. I would work in other areas, but something always drew me back to hospitality.

One of the barriers, or perceived barriers to be more accurate, about working in hospitality is that it's not perceived as a "serious" profession. That notion affected me and for a while took me away from entertaining any idea of a career in hospitality, even though I always enjoyed it when I was working in the industry.

Another factor that inhibited me, particularly from going into management in the hospitality industry, was that I always believed myself to be a people-pleaser. In management that's fatal, you just cannot please everyone all the time. I felt that I didn't want to be stuck between staff and bosses, so I shied away from it.

For several years, I wanted to be my own boss. I went to college and studied and practiced counselling, which was fascinating and provided a brilliant insight into people and what makes them tick. I seriously considered setting up my own counselling practice.

Then, one day, my husband Alex, who works at the *Battlefield Rest*, a popular Italian restaurant on the southside of Glasgow, came home and told me Marco, the proprietor, was wanting to sell the business, and that changed everything.

Alex: I would never have seen myself running a restaurant when I was young. After I left school, I went to university to study medical biology. During this time, I worked as a barman in a pub. I found working in the pub both far more structured and fun than my course at university, so after two years I dropped out.

A while later, I landed a job as a waiter at a fast-food restaurant in Glasgow's West End. A lot of students went there but also people from all walks of life and nationalities. I was broadening my horizons and picked up a lot of experience in a fast moving, very busy restaurant where no two days were ever the same.

I had two friends from my school days who were working as chefs at the *Battlefield Rest* which was a well-regarded and popular restaurant in the Southside of the city. They let me know that the restaurant was looking for staff. It was closer to home, and I knew that it would be run on more professional lines than the often-chaotic environment of a fast-food diner. It was the right time for me to make a move, I thought. I'd picked up a lot of skills in fast food, but it wasn't a career choice for me.

Glasgow, despite its size, is in many ways a village and people who dine out a lot or work in bars or restaurants form a kind of community. I still get customers who either live in the West End or have moved to the south side, come into the *Rest*, and do a double take when they see me. You can see them thinking: "Is that not that guy who worked in that diner in the West End?" But it gives you some measure of the impression you've made on people and that's always the hallmark of a good waiter.

I'd often thought about owning and managing my own restaurant. At every venue I've worked at in hospitality I've always wondered how the bosses or owners got to that position, how did they start it up, how was it funded. They don't teach you any of that anywhere.

During the period I've been working at the *Rest,* I'd been offered the chance to take over and run a café in the Battlefield area not far from the *Rest*. But I didn't know how to go about making an offer or how I could go about raising the funds, so that opportunity slipped by.

Another time there was a derelict outbuilding in a nearby park which was up for sale, and I thought that would be a great place for a café. Sure enough, it was snapped up and six months later it was a thriving café and newsagents. I'd missed the chance yet again because I didn't know what to do.

I'd been working at the *Rest* for five years when Marco approached me in confidence and told me he was considering selling the business and asked me would I be interested, and if I was, to make him an offer. I went home and told Jen.

Taking over at Battlefield

Jen: When Alex told me that Marco was selling up and offered Alex the chance to buy the business, I said to him straightaway: 'Make him an offer. I'll support you and we'll work together as a partnership.' I was excited and loved the idea of Alex and I being our own bosses.

Remember, I said I was a people-pleaser. So, for me working in a restaurant, serving people good quality food, providing them with a good time, ticked a lot of boxes for me.

The downside was, we were just coming out of covid into a world of uncertainty, especially in hospitality. The *Rest*, I well knew from Alex, had come out of it with its head above water, but there was still a lot of anxiety. Because I'd worked in a variety of places previously, I had a lot of contacts such as accountants, lawyers and other professionals who could provide me with solid, practical advice and I didn't flinch from asking for that advice.

Personality wise, I now felt I was a lot stronger and that was greatly assisted by my counselling training and experience where I could bounce ideas and issues off people in a safe environment. I realised I was in a much better place where I was no longer trying to please everyone but could make decisions and be assertive. The upshot was I had no doubts I could do this. Plus, I am a hard worker, not scared to get my hands dirty and put in a shift which is essential in this trade.

Alex and I discussed it fully, weighing up all the options. Our conclusion: Go for it! The chance to run a place like the *Rest* doesn't come up every day! Alex went back and made an offer to Marco which he accepted.

Alex: When I told Jen Marco had offered me the chance to buy the business, she replied instantly: 'make him an offer'. And I replied, truthfully, I didn't know where to start.

This period of uncertainty on my part lasted for a while with Marco persistently enquiring when I was going to make him an offer and time marching on to the point where he was going to sell on the open market and another opportunity would slip by. Jen became frustrated and eventually gave me an ultimatum: either tell him straight, you won't be making an offer and drop it completely or make him an offer. 'If you don't know where to start,' she said, 'then offer him a tenner.'

Back in the early 1990s Marco had bought the abandoned building that became the *Battlefield Rest* from the council for a nominal sum of £1 before transforming it into the bustling restaurant it is today. Offering him £10 was actually ten times greater than he'd bought it for!

Anyway, that began the discussions and proceedings that lasted about eighteen months and culminated in Jen and I agreeing a deal to buy the business from Marco.

One big advantage I had was that I'd worked there for five years. I knew the business, how popular it was, and I was familiar with the substantial and loyal customer base who I'd got to know well, and they'd got to know me. That was important for continuity once word got around Marco was selling up. All-in-all then I had a good start. Not many people in this game have that advantage.

It also helped that in the preceding eighteen months I'd taken on more and more responsibilities in the restaurant. So, while I'm not going to deny I was a bit nervous and jittery when Jen and I took over on the first of December 2022, I wasn't walking into a situation I knew nothing about.

Jen: Our first day in charge of the restaurant was first of December 2022. Yes, that's right, slap bang in the build-up to Christmas, the busiest season for any restaurant. Of course, it was nerve-wracking. Alex and I agreed that we wouldn't make any radical changes immediately. We'd take our time, and our priority was to get through Christmas. Above all, keep the customers happy.

Marco had taken the wise decision not to publicise that he was selling the business. Since it opened back in the early 90s', the *Rest* has been associated with Marco who built it up into what it has become. We all agreed that people, not least the customers, might become apprehensive that he was leaving if it was done too quickly. The rumour-mill can be dangerous for any hospitality venue about to change hands.

We all agreed it would be far better that Alex and I bed in and make the transition gradual. So, when people did become aware, it was a done deal, and the business was running just as well under the new owners. I think it's safe to say now after all this time, that strategy has worked. We're still incredibly busy, all our regular customers have stayed with us, and the world knows that Marco no longer runs the place and that's been accepted (though he's still a fixture, waitering in the restaurant several days a week).

After that first day we'd taken over, when I arrived back home that night all I could think was about paying the invoices the next day, what was the plan for tomorrow and this and that. What I've realised since is that planning too much never works out. It's often a lot better just to be in the present and use your experience and knowledge to take what comes.

It hit home when we got through Christmas and had a couple of days off during the festive holiday break. We thought Ok, we've got through Christmas, but now comes the lean period of January and how do we deal with that? Alex and I decided we'd hold a staff meeting and have an honest, frank discussion with staff about what was going right and what needed changing, and what they would like to see changing.

We've been in charge for over a year now, and, if I'm honest, I don't feel really there's been much difference. The main reason for that is the *Rest* is a successful operation that ticks over, it works, its popular and always busy and you risk a lot trying to tinker and mess about with that. A lot of that is down to the excellent and experienced staff.

If you want to use an analogy, we've inherited a very powerful, fast and reliable car. Our job is to steer it rightly and only make any changes that will keep it on the road.

Alex: From the first day Jen and I took charge, things have gone well. Having Marco stay on as a staff member has helped. As word started to emerge that he was no longer the owner, his continued presence in the building provided that level of comfort and assurance to customers that there was a smooth handover and transition in progress. The staff have been fantastic too. Most of them have been here for years and I've got to know them well and that does help.

I'm often asked how it feels to have your ex-boss, i.e., Marco, working for you now. It's turned out ok so far, but on one recent Saturday night when he was working, he came up to me and said: 'you need to sort out a problem at one of the tables.' I was halfway across the room to the table in question when I stopped, went back up to Marco with a grin on my face and said: 'I pay you. *You* sort it out!' And we both laughed.

Jen and I are a partnership and I find her motivating. The two of us are looking forward to the future and continuing to make *Battlefield Rest* the great, popular, and dynamic restaurant it has become. One great responsibility Jane and I have, as indeed did Marco before us, is the awareness that a lot of people's happiness are resting on you. That first date, birthdays, anniversaries, staff nights out and so on, people are depending on you to ensure the atmosphere, food and service are right to make it a memorable night for them. If I get that wrong, which I can assure you I don't intend to, I'll be getting chased out of Battlefield, if not Glasgow.

Reflections on women in leading roles in hospitality

Jen: There does seem to be few women in charge of restaurants, though there are more female head chefs emerging. But I do think there's a lot of women behind the scenes that have a strong influence in how restaurants are run and managed. The *Rest* is a good example of that where there had always been a strong partnership between Marco and his wife, Yellena, and now with Alex and me. I think you'll find there's a lot of that in this business if you dig deep enough.

Another factor possibly inhibiting women from entering the trade, and I've heard this a few times, is how can you start a family in the hospitality trade with the long hours and all the stresses and strains? I would argue back why not? If you don't try it, you'll never find out.

Incidents from the past

Jen: I was once working in a private member's club in Glasgow and my friend Colin, who was front of house, and I decided to play a practical joke on the kitchen which backfired on me. I was twenty-one at the time, so I'm pleading youth and innocence. There was a dumb waiter which led from the kitchen to the dining room in the club. We thought it would be a laugh if I fitted myself into the dumb waiter, Colin lowered me down to the kitchen, the kitchen staff opened the hatch and, hey presto, I popped out and gave them the shock of their lives. The problem was we hadn't realised that all the kitchen staff had left and gone home as it was the end of the day.

I got lowered down and when I was level with the kitchen waited for someone to open the door, But, of course, nobody came because no one was there. After a few minutes in the confined space and pitch darkness of the dumbwaiter I started hollering:

'Hello, anyone there? Get me out, please!'

I became increasingly desperate, and it must have been a good twenty-to-thirty minutes before Colin thought: 'That's strange, she's taking ages,' before he finally came downstairs to the kitchen and rescued me. By the time he did so I was panicking. No pun intended but it was a dumb idea not to check that the kitchen staff were still on duty when you're going to carry out a stunt like that!

Alex: In hospitality, you never know who's coming through your door next, so never judge people. I remember when working at the fast-food diner in the West End this woman came in one day by herself. She was a quirky looking lady, and I got a strange vibe from her. I took her order for a salmon salad and made sure I served her it. The minute I put it in front of her she let out this scream and shouted: 'No egg! No egg!' She looked terrified. I immediately took it away (she hadn't mentioned anything, I was sure, about eggs when I took her order), binned it and the kitchen made a fresh salmon salad, minus, of course, the eggs.

When it was ready, I took the salad out to her again. She was fine with the food this time. This was twenty years ago when most people used cash to pay their bills. That woman paid with a private bank card, not your conventional credit or debit card. Her card went through with no problem, and she left. I was curious and looked her up online. It transpired she was an editor at *Vogue* magazine in New York. I would never have guessed that's who she was. From a top-flight magazine in New York to a wee lane in Glasgow, you never know who you're going to get through the door.

Advice

Jen: Network. Find people who you can speak to, who've got experience of the trade and pick their brains. I would say, yes, the hours are crazy, the stresses can be enormous, but the feeling of reward, of satisfaction from running your own restaurant is incredible. You're working for yourself, you're you own boss and when it all works out, nothing can beat it. Once you've taken all the advice and weighed up the pros and cons, go for it!

Alex: If you see an opportunity, have a go. If you don't, you'll always wonder what could have been. But make sure you judge it carefully and do a lot of preparation. Don't dive in. A lot of people have with dire results.

Jen's favourite dish: When I was young, after travelling to Ireland all day on a coach to see my grandparents, as soon as I arrived my grandmother would serve up this delicious homemade chicken noodle soup with these incredible tasting mini pizzas. Heaven!

Also, my mom's mince and potatoes, or mince n' tatties, as it's better known in Scotland. Absolutely scrumptious!

Alex's favourite dish: My wife's lasagne. I ask her to make me it a lot. She takes a day-and-a-half to cook it, but the result is outstanding!

Jen's favourite wine: A red Poppone. Best wine I've ever tasted.

Alex's favourite wine: Vallone. We recently had a promotion for it in the *Rest* and every member of staff bought a bottle after having a glass of it. You can't say better than that.

14. GUY COWAN: KEEPING IT SIMPLE

For fourteen years Guy Cowan ran the very popular Guy's Restaurant in Glasgow. Before that he had a remarkable career, including catering for major film productions and feeding top movie stars. Here he reveals all.

Beginnings

My father was the son of a Lithuanian rabbi while my mother was of Irish stock. They attended medical school at Glasgow University training as doctors. When they decided to marry, they eloped, and my father was cut off by his father. The old man even held a Shiva house for my father where the loss of someone close through death is mourned. It wouldn't happen now but that was those days. My mother's family became my dad's family.

I remember dad having a distinctly different diet from my mother. She liked simple food, but dad enjoyed more exotic food. In the early 1960s' I can recall mum making dad a poached whole onion in white sauce and dad devouring it. Dad would often arrive home with tins of octopus, strings of saveloys and sweet and sour bread. That's when I became a voracious eater and loved food.

My dad died when I was eight, leaving my mother to bring up six kids on her own. I was sent to boarding school at the former St Joseph's College in Dumfries, which was run by the Marist Brothers, incidentally the order that started Glasgow Celtic football club. I mention that because in 1969 I had my picture taken with the legendary Celtic manager, Jock Stein, when he came to visit the school.

Anyway, the food was atrocious at St Joseph's. I couldn't believe how bad it was. I survived by eating straight out of cans, cold. A school chum told me that cans couldn't be interfered with, not least by the school kitchen, so, therefore all I needed was a can opener and hey presto, I'd scoff right from the can. To this day I still eat Heinz ravioli straight from the can when I'm low. Don't ever tell my Italian friends!

Another survival mechanism at St Joseph's were the weekly visits from family members on Sundays. You were allowed to leave the school grounds with visitors on a Sunday and mum would bring down bacon and egg sandwiches on toasted plain bread which I would eat in the car before going for breakfast – yes that's right, breakfast *after* the bacon and eggs – at the Cairndale Hotel. Then we went onto a magical place called *Bruno's* a family-owned restaurant for lunch where we would be served by Bruno himself. It's still there. I went back a few years ago and as a young waiter served my food, I asked about Bruno; he lit up and said: 'oh yes, Bruno, he was my great-grandfather!' Every now and then I return there; must be the longest association I've had with any restaurant!

We'd head for dinner in a tiny Chinese place called *Go Sun*, the very first place I ever ate shiitake mushrooms and was introduced to salad cream on my fried rice - remember this was the late 60's' - before finishing off the day at *Dante's Café* for a wee plate of chips dripping with salt, vinegar, and salad cream. I just gorged the whole day, so I could survive on cans for the rest of the week. Thank goodness for my family and those Sunday visits!

Despite the school's restrictions, by the age of 13 we were able to sneak out and get served alcohol in *The Nith Hotel*. Now, most boy's role models for a wee swally are their fathers, and that usually means, in Scotland at least anyway, beer. But mine was my mother as my father had passed away. So, whereas all the other boys were ordering pints of beer, I was buying glasses of sherry. I got a lot of stick for that!

I left St Joseph's under a large cloud before being sent to my final seat of learning - there had been many, schools and I never did get on. I ended up dogging school and working in a place called *Slack Shack* in Glasgow city centre selling jeans. Next to it was a shop named *Ritz* which took orders for platform sole boots – it was the beginning of the glam rock era, and I managed to get a job there too. Sex, drugs, rock and roll with several late night visits to burger vans. I was a top shagger!

Eventually I had to get sensible and started working in the family grocery business for a few years. My grandfather, on my mother's side, was John Curley who built up an impressive chain of grocery shops. I worked there for a few years, but there were tensions around the business within the family.

It was a typical story that happens in a lot of family businesses. The first generation build it up, then the next generation takes over, no one gets on and everyone has different ideas about how it should be run.

One night the family held a meeting, agreed we'd all get out, close all the premises, pay the bills, share out everything that was left, and everyone would go their own way. And that's what happened.

Setting up a deli

I struck out on my own and in 1983 opened a deli in Byres Road, one of the busiest streets in Glasgow's West End. It was sited just along from a very famous landmark Glasgow pub called the *Rubaiyat*. The reason I mention that is because that was where my mum and dad would meet for dates before they were married. It was a sad day for quality and tradition when it was reduced to a sterile plastic pub called *Finlay's*.

At the deli, I sold a wide variety of foods that were difficult to obtain in Glasgow in those days; there was no Waitrose or stores like that then. I got involved with a company called Alan Porter Provisions who every week brought over a van filled with produce from the famous Parisian Rungis market. These were treasures like morels, foie gras en croute, white truffles, and little glass jars of French yoghurts which you couldn't get elsewhere in the country. My deli was quite unique, and I built up an astonishing customer following.

Then, one day after just over six months' trading, in walks an official from Glasgow District Council, who were my landlords. He told me there was subsidence in the building and I was going to have to close for at least six months with immediate effect. I retorted, 'You must be joking. This doesn't just happen overnight; you must have known about this! Why didn't you tell my lawyer before I signed up to the rental agreement?' The reply I eventually received from the council was: 'Your lawyer didn't ask the question.' I had no option but to shut up shop.

Going rural and oriental

I was introduced to a very posh real estate developer from Belgravia with a major project transforming the centre of Penrith, a sleepy agricultural town in the north of England on the edge of the Lake District, into a delightfully modern little gem. There was a farming supplies and grocery business in the centre of town called J.J. Graham which had been around for 200 years. My new friend asked me to help transform this purveyor of guano, seeds and hams into a mini Harrod's style food hall in the Lake District. Given my experience in the grocery business and the deli, I accepted the challenge. It was a roaring success for the first two-and-a-half years, but the last six months were not great, I fell out with my Eton Row chum. Let's not mention Prince Philip, Perrier Jouet and the Golf GTi.

Amongst the many friends I made down there were a very colourful married couple, who were the tenants of a charming wee pub called the *Punchbowl* in the village of Askham in the Lake District National Park just outside Penrith. The pub had a fully fitted kitchen in the rear, but the only food they served was typical pub fare: fish and chips, burgers, toasties and so on. There was also a lovely dining room that wasn't being used. I suggested to the couple, why not open the dining room, and turn it into a restaurant? They agreed.

Around this time Marco Pierre White was a rising star and the talk of food town. My friend's wife and I booked a table at White's place, *Harveys*, in London, for a Saturday night to see what was on offer and what ideas we could pick up for the new restaurant in Askham.

However, on the Friday night before, at the suggestion of another friend we went to the *Red Pepper*, a Szechuan restaurant in West London. We were blown away with the food. I'd never tasted anything like that in my life. It was spectacular. We cancelled the booking at *Harveys* and went to another Szechuan restaurant on the Saturday. It wasn't quite as good, but we got the bug to turn the dining room into Askham's first Chinese restaurant.

That Sunday morning, we scoured Chinatown and bought all the best and proper equipment and ingredients: woks, pots, pans, oils, seeds, spices and other essentials required, also a copy of Yan Kit's *Classic Chinese Cookery*, to which I still refer. Within two weeks we converted the dining room, prepared the kitchen, and opened the restaurant despite never having cooked Chinese food for more than four people in my life.

Askham was in the middle of nowhere. There was no internet, so apart from the locals, it was all word-of-mouth. Nowadays, within two days of opening, they'll know about you in Hong Kong because of social media. Over the next few months, we built up a good trade. One day a chap came in who'd been fell walking and ordered dinner. A short time later this chap sent me a copy of the weekly column he wrote for a Leeds newspaper. He was a food critic and restaurant reviewer; he'd mentioned us in his column. It was a great piece with a brilliant headline that read:

"*Want to eat Chinese food in the Lake District cooked by a Glaswegian who's never been to China? Come to…*" That helped put us on the map, and I've still got that clipping.

It didn't last, despite the success. The following September, the couple gave up the tenancy and I came back to Glasgow. I wasn't sure what I wanted to do. This was now the mid-1980s, but I didn't think Glasgow was ready for gastropubs at that time. Catering in most Glasgow pubs was still crisps and a pie with brown sauce!

Catering for the stars

I knew a girl who worked as the head chef in a West-End pub. She suggested that I work there for a while to get a feel for what it was like to work in a kitchen that was part of a pub. I worked there for three months, but the food was mediocre and not up to the standard I wanted to be associated with. This was no reflection on my friend, the head chef. The kitchen and menu were controlled and dictated by the parent company who had zero interest in culinary flair, and she was severely restricted in the quality and style of food she could prepare and serve.

Around this time there was a movie being made in Glasgow called Silent Scream directed by David Hayman and starring Iain Glen, Julie Graham and Robert Carlyle amongst many other talented players. The catering company on the locations with them was a Dublin outfit and they'd been told in no uncertain terms by the production company they had one week to "clean up their act" or they were off the site.

The head chef for the catering company had a nickname: Maggot. Believe me, you don't want your head chef to be known as Maggot! This Maggot guy happened to drink in the West End bar I'd been working in and one day got speaking to my friend the head chef. He said he was looking for a chef "urgently." She recommended me and gave him my number.

I had a look. The kitchen was a seven-and-half tonne truck with the hygiene levels of the toilets at Woodstock. I accepted their job offer on condition that before I came on board the kitchen was gleaming. That was the Friday. By the Monday it was like an operating theatre; dazzlingly sterile. I brought my menus and ingredients, on my first day crew members commented they were amazed fresh vegetables were available for the first time.

I gave Maggot lists of things to purchase and when he tried to foist cheaper alternatives on me, I told him firmly: 'Take that back. I'm not cooking with that!' He soon got the message. At the end of that first week, we got the thumbs up, the caterers could stay on as long as I was there.

Towards the end of nine weeks filming, I got a heads up. A new production, The Big Man starring Liam Neeson and Billy Connolly, was about to roll into town and the company were going to be offered the catering contract on condition that I was kept on as head chef. Sure enough, they offered me the position. I said only if I got double the money. Right away they agreed. I should have held out for treble!

The catering company was based in Dublin, they'd nobody in Glasgow where more and more films were getting made. So, I suggested buying in, I'd be a partner - essentially their man in Scotland. They demanded way too much money. I gave them an ultimatum: lower the price or I'll set up my own operation. Go ahead they responded, never believing I would, I did.

I bought a single-decker bus in North Wales and brought it back to Glasgow. With the invaluable help of my father-in-law who'd been vice-chair of the engineering company, the Weir Group, and was a brilliant handyman, who did all the plumbing and other jobs that I just fail miserably with, and my mother-in-law, who planned out the kitchen, we were ready to go. I came up with the name for the company: *Reel Food* with the tagline: *Real Food for Reel People*. It soon became Scotland's number one location kitchen and go to caterer.

And it wasn't just Scotland. We worked all over the UK, especially London and I provided the catering on such films as Trainspotting, Spice Girls, Bridget Jones, and the Constant Gardener to name just a few. I fed a host of big names, getting a kiss from Jennifer Aniston and a cuddle from Cameron Diaz. I even ended up feeding Mick Jagger, a personal hero of mine, for twelve weeks.

Jagger played a transvestite night club hostess in Berlin café society; the film was called Bent. On the first day we saw a whole convoy of vehicles coming into the unit base; Mick was arriving. There were folk holding out umbrellas for Mick and his entourage and other folk holding out umbrellas for the folk with umbrellas while others were scattering roses on the ground.

Filming was at night, turning over at 6pm. I thought this is going to be a nightmare, not with the main man, but the folk around them. Sure enough, this girl approached me. She identified herself as one of Mick's PAs and ordered everything from the menu. We delivered this vast array of food to Mick's trailer.

Early the next morning, about 5am we're getting on with the breakfast prep, I sensed someone behind me, it was Jumping Jack Flash himself. He said: 'Thought I'd introduce myself.' Tongue-in-cheek I asked him: 'Who are you?' He laughed, then said: 'Do me a favour. In future, please come to me and tell me what there is to eat.'

I've still got the bottle of champagne and faint handwritten thank you note he gave me in his trailer.

I took over the contract on the London end of the film Derailed with Clive Owen and Jennifer Aniston. Previously I'd catered a couple of movies in Scotland that Clive had starred in, the guy's a joy. The original caterers on Derailed were so bad that he'd said to the film makers: 'Get this guy down from Scotland.' That's how I'd got that contract.

It was around the time when Jennifer Aniston was very publicly breaking up with Brad Pitt, she must have been under a lot of stress and pressure. She was great. No diva behaviour, no tantrums, professional to the last. On her final day in London, she came in to see me and said: 'Thanks for feeding me,' and gave me a big cuddle and a kiss. I didn't wash for weeks after that.

Overseeing the catering for movies is great, for young guys. It's also highly stressful, often requiring up to 18-hour shifts for weeks. The final straw for me was when I fell afoul of a US director. After 15 weeks on the road and with just a week to go her daughter arrived and proceeded to party till four in the morning. Her mother wanted her up at five, but she claimed she was unwell due to food poisoning. I got the blame. A doctor was called to examine her, and he told me it most certainly wasn't food poisoning, but the director was adamant, I was to blame. The producer came up to me and said: 'sorry, you're off the job, she wants you out.'

I took them to court, well at least started the process, they made me an offer I couldn't refuse, paid my legal fees and gave me a letter of apology and retracted the original slur.

I realised it was time to move on.

Back home and opening *Guy's restaurant*

Back in Glasgow, Colin Beattie, charming and gifted owner of the *Oran Mor* bar and nightclub in the West End, mentioned to me he was renting out a place on North Street, just to the west of the city-centre. There was a bar upstairs, kitchen and restaurant downstairs. I looked over it, liked what I saw said 'yes' and opened it with a simple menu. I served only the food that I liked to eat which is why I called it *Guy's* because this is what Guy eats. We built up a good following and hit on a good formula.

Sadly, there were issues with the rather frumpy landlady of the bar above us. She was so miserable even her dogs topped themselves!

Like Elvis, Guy left the building, for a spot in the Merchant City and *Guy's* Mark 2 was born. The new place opened in the mid-nineties, and we didn't look back. We were in a good central location in a fast-growing part of town. My previous contacts in the film world proved invaluable and quite a few celebrities I'd catered for or knew popped in which always earned good publicity. They included Robert Englund, Ray Winstone, Ken Stott, Ewan McGregor and Bob Hoskins.

Bob Hoskins had a great sense of mischief. We had a similar appearance. On the set of Last Orders, he came in just before lunch service, demanded that I give him an apron and my glasses, which he put on, and then as customers filed in for lunch, proceeded to serve them. What a guy! A lovely man dearly missed.

Guy's opened for fourteen very successful years. We became a landmark on the Glasgow dining scene, and we were always busy. As always in this game, there were many challenges. I have many memories although these two incidents stick out.

One Mother's Day we had a slightly odd family in. The mother was in her late 80's and had travelled down from Aberdeen to be with her family. Unknown to us, she suffered from some condition and was violently ill, being very sick in the toilet. My wife went to help her. The poor woman had been sick all over herself, so my wife helped her to change into a spare set of my whites, which just about fitted her.

We phoned an ambulance and received some strange looks from the paramedics when they arrived as they took this old lady dressed in a chef's outfit to the hospital. But what was even stranger was the reaction of the family. None of them went to the hospital with their mother. They just sat there. When my wife and I said to them: 'Your mother's going to the hospital!' they calmly said: 'But our dinners just getting served. We'll see our mother after.' Honestly, as they say, there's nowt stranger than folk.

Another occasion, this very bright and successful customer was having his thirtieth birthday party. He'd hired the entire restaurant. The guest of honour was Alex Salmond, then Scotland's First Minister and the guest speaker was the comedian, Rory Bremmer.

Because the First Minister was going to be in attendance, there was a lot of cloak and dagger business with his security people. They wanted to know where the back exits were and who had keys for this and that and so on. Alex Salmond's driver started talking to me and said he'd heard that 'you do nice steak pies. We're driving to Aberdeen. You couldn't give us some steak pies, could you?'

I said I would provide them, but I needed the dishes back. I made him up half a dozen steak pies, but I never got the *bloody dishes back*!

Over the years, quite a few customers have become friends. Just recently I catered at the fortieth birthday for the son of one my former customers, which was delightful.

For all the stress, strain, and challenges, that's one of the many pleasures of being in this trade, meeting so many interesting and lovely people.

Advice

If you're thinking about a life in the restaurant business, please consider the following:

- It really is a hands-on career, certainly until you are established, which may take years. It's hard but satisfying work.
- There are highs but there are lows, be prepared to ride the storms.
- Cook what you like to eat but know your audience.
- Some weeks, you may be the only sucker who didn't get paid.
- Remember, it's a business, don't give away too many comps.
- You'll spend more time with your passion than with your family.

If none of this daunts you then you are right for the job, good luck.

P.S. Don't let anyone borrow your knives!!!

Guy's favourite dishes:

I've always said that if I was stranded on a desert island, I would like to have ten of my favourite dishes. They are, in no particular order:

Bacon and eggs on toasted plain bread with lashings of salted French butter.

Cheese pudding

Spaghetti with meat sauce or truffle or porcini

Ravioli with any of the above sauces

Any curry from the *Mother India* group, although minced lamb and peas is life changing.

Proper Peking Duck

All Dim Sum

Mince n' tatties

Breaded haddock pan fried in pure peanut oil

Tournedos Rossini

Guy's favourite drinks:

I no longer drink alcohol, but I used to love Special Brew which was known in Glasgow as '*who you looking at?*' with a Grouse chaser.

Nowadays a good alcohol-free beer or gin or cocktail. Although if I'm drinking water, give me San Pellegrino or Aqua Panna, not the stuff oot the taps….

15. NATALINO CELINO: FOUNDING A GLASGOW LEGEND

Celino's Delicatessen and Trattoria in Glasgow's east end has served satisfied customers for decades. Just recently expanded, the founder, Natalino, reveals how he went from a farmhand to becoming the owner of one of Glasgow's best loved restaurants.

Beginnings

My family were poor farmers as were most people where I came from in Italy. So, my grandfather on my father's side went to work in America for five years and then worked in England for a further seven years before going back to Italy. With the money he managed to earn and save, he was able to buy land in his home village. In fact, he became the second biggest landowner and built a big house for the family. While he was working in England, he brought his wife over, and she became pregnant and gave birth to my uncle who was born in Plymouth in 1936 before going back to Italy.

My uncle went back to Britain, to Glasgow when he was older. He lived in the West End and raised a family of eight children. The family owned a shop in Partick and settled there. Back in Italy the rest of the family wanted to come to Scotland and both my brother and sister came across occasionally to work with my uncle, so he was the pull factor drawing us across.

Even though I wanted to come to Glasgow my first job was at an international hotel in Zurich, Switzerland for six months. This was back in 1960 when I was 18. The reason I went to Switzerland was because a lot of my friends were going there; it was a trend. I'd had no previous experience of hospitality and was straight off a farm in Italy. The difference between the luxury of the big, flash hotel in Zurich and home was massive. Back home my folks had no running water, only a well where they drew water from whereas at the hotel, I could shower twice a day.

Moving to Scotland: From farm hand to café owner

I had a short stay back in Italy and finally came over to Glasgow in 1962. But I didn't work in the city at first. In fact, I spent four years on various farms in Lanarkshire and near Cumbernauld. Coming from a farming background, I knew my way around. On my first farm I was milking 80 cows a day and this only months after that stint at the luxury hotel in Zurich: what a contrast!

The farming life ended when I my met my wife at a café in the east end of Glasgow. It was called the *Swallow Cafe* in the Dennistoun part of the east-end of the city and was owned by her family. We started seeing each other, fell in love and decided to get married. But there was a condition imposed by my future father-in-law. If I wanted to continue seeing her and get married, I had to work in the shop. You see my future mother-in-law wouldn't allow her daughter to go anywhere, so she was confined to the shop.

I went along with my father-in-law's wishes, left the farm, and started working in the café. This was situated in a very busy street called Alexandra Parade, known locally as the Parade. If I'm being honest since I started working in that café, my wife and I have spent all of our working lives on the Parade.

After we married, I worked full-time in the café. My father-in-law had two shops: the café and a fish and chip shop nearby. He agreed to let my wife and I take over the café while he focused on the fish and chip shop. We ran the café for three years. It was typical of its time selling ice creams, soft drinks, and the like. Then my wife became pregnant. Working in the café involved long hours and I didn't want the two of us doing that when a baby was on the way.

We gave up the café and bought a shop selling fruit on the Parade. That allowed us to shut the shop about six and have a home life with our first child. After three years we sold the shop and bought a corner shop, again in the Parade, and transformed it into a very successful and popular fruit shop and florists. Despite being confined to her father's shops my wife had a good head for business and the two of us were good florists. We had that shop for twenty-eight years and raised a family over those years.

After all that time and with the kids growing up, we decided to sell the shop to a local bookie. My brother-in-law had moved to Brighton, and we went down there for a few months to visit him. While there, we looked at this unit in Hove next to Brighton and thought we could turn it into a takeaway and sell pizzas and lasagne and so on. We agreed an unsigned contract with the property owner and came back to Glasgow for a few months.

Becoming Celino's

While home my wife took ill and was in a lot of pain. We went to the doctor and to our astonishment she told us my wife was pregnant. It had been fourteen years since my wife had her last baby, which was a difficult pregnancy and she'd been told she couldn't have any more children. But here she was pregnant again!

That changed everything. Brighton was off and thank goodness we hadn't signed that contract for the unit down there. My wife gave birth to a heathy baby girl, our last child Maria.

That was great but I felt lost without having a business to run and no income coming in. Then I came across an empty unit which is now part of *Celino's* on Alexandra Parade. I took it over and turned it into another shop selling fruit and flowers. We were back in business.

Soon, though, I realised that the flowers weren't selling as well as they had previously. In addition, people's shopping habits were changing with the rise of the supermarkets. That's where they were buying their fruit. I knew I had to change tack, or I'd go out of business. So, I started selling sandwiches and soups which sold very well, and the business rapidly picked up.

I decided to buy the unit next door and turned that into a deli selling pastas and salmi. The two units became the basis of Celino's which has been on the Parade ever since.

The shop is now spread across three units, and we've got a sit-in café section which also does good business. Our takeaway deli has always done a great trade, particularly over the lunch period with all the shops and businesses nearby.

The key to keeping a successful business like this going is always to serve good quality food and keep the customers happy. If a regular customer I know and trust comes in here saying 'that meat you sold me at the deli was poor,' I won't argue with them, and I'll replace the meat.

One big change I've noticed is the difference in attitude towards Italian people. We were definitely not top of the class years ago and there was quite a level of hostility or resentment towards us. That's changed completely and there's nothing like that now; certainly, my children have never experienced that.

Another way you can see this is by how much Italian food has become a staple part of people's normal shopping habits or dining in restaurants rather than just fast food as it used to be. Lasagne and pasta are now as popular, if not more popular, as mince and tatties in Scotland. At the bowling club I'm a member of, people there are getting good quality Italian dishes such as tagliatelle with two slices of fillet on top and a bottle of wine for up to £40 delivered to their homes every Friday. That would have been unheard of even 20 years ago.

However, the rise of the Chinese and Indian fast food and takeaway shops, as well as all the burger places, have impacted badly on the fish and chip shops that were mainly run by Italians. The days when fish and chip shops were always open past nine at night are gone.

I'm fully retired now and delighted to see how *Celino's* on the Parade is still doing so well and popular and run very well by my sons and daughters. In 2017 we opened a new site in the West End in Partick, also called *Celino's* which has proved to be a great success as well.

Now I can put my feet up and relax apart from looking after the grandchildren a few days a week, knowing the business is in safe hands. Long may it last.

Advice
Hard work, determination, sweat, keeping your head and feet on the ground and taking the good times with the bad. Always sell good quality and keep your customers happy and that'll help you on the road to success.

Celino's favourite dish: My mother's lasagne cooked in an oven next to the fire over charcoal and burnt logs served in a terracotta dish. Stupendous!

Cellino's favourite wine: Merlot, Chianti

16. CHRIS MARTINOLLI, SHINING A LIGHT THE ITALIAN WAY: THE MAN BEHIND LA LANTERNA

Think of an old-world Italian restaurant and La Lanterna in Glasgow City Centre comes immediately to mind. Serving beautiful traditional dishes in a distinctive ambience, Chris Martinolli, co-owner (along with his business partner, multi-award-winning head chef, Luca Conreno) explains the ingredients that keeps this lantern shining brightly.

Beginnings

My mother was English, and my father was Italian who moved to Glasgow in the 1960s and worked as a chef at a hotel outside Glasgow not far from Loch Lomond. He moved from there to become head chef of a famous Italian restaurant called *Ferrari's* in Sauchiehall Street in the city centre. There he met his future business partner and they decided to open a new restaurant in another part of the city centre besides Glasgow Central railway station. That restaurant was called *La Lanterna* and opened in September 1970. It's been open there under that name for over 50 years which makes it one of the oldest Italian restaurants in Glasgow. I took over from my father with my business partner in early 1998, so I've run it for over 25 years.

I was around the restaurant from an early age. I always knew I'd work in hospitality and studied catering and hotel management in college. After that I worked in Italy, but my dad started suffering poor health and I came back to lend a hand in the restaurant. Very soon, however, Dad's health got worse, and he could no longer come into the restaurant. My original intention was to run it for a few months and sell it. But as I settled into working there and realised how busy and popular it was, I thought I could run it on my own and make the changes I thought were necessary to improve it and make it even better.

My dad's business partner was still around and came into the restaurant occasionally. He was resistant to the changes I was suggesting. Understandably so when a young guy at 25 is telling an older guy at 68 how to run the place he's operated successfully for 25 years! We sat down, negotiated and eventually I bought his side of the business. I didn't want to run it on my own and I found a business partner in the chef at the restaurant, a chap named Luca, who's now the head chef. We formed a partnership and took over, pushed it forward and slowly made changes.

Luca and I had to be careful at first. We'd inherited an ageing customer base, so any changes had to be gradual. But we got there with the help of a younger staff without alienating anyone.

The classic restaurant

I would say the city centre *La Lanterna* restaurant has developed into is a "classic restaurant" which means an old-world diner with a timeless ambience. They're warm and not too stuffy or formal. You can relax in them. There's friendly staff who are welcoming and get to know the customers. But they've got standards in terms of the food and even the way the staff are dressed. I think there's about five of these mid-level, mid-market "classic restaurants" left in Glasgow. Especially since covid, the café bars, the diners, the small plates venues now overwhelmingly dominate the dining scene in the city.

At the higher end you've got a few upmarket, fine dining restaurants, some with the Michelin Star, which add a lot of prestige to the city, but your average Glaswegian isn't going to be dining there every week. That will be mainly for a special occasion. There's a market for classic restaurants and the city-centre site caters for that.

Maintaining success

We've maintained this classic restaurant as I now call it and it's been consistently successful and I'm proud that I've carried on my father's legacy. Part of maintaining that legacy and success is adapting the menu. While it's important to have some traditional dishes that you're well known for, it's also vital that you refresh the menu and it's not just this static set of items you're offering. People like a combination of the new and the old; it attracts them. Too many places have stuck to what was a successful menu and never changed with nothing new on offer. People get weary of that and move on.

The other vital element is your staff. As the manager or proprietor, you cannot be out there all the time. It's vital that waitering staff are polite, helpful, attentive and embody the business's values. If the customers adore the waiter that served them, then that completes the quality of the food and the atmosphere. On the other hand, if that waiter is indifferent to them or has a bad attitude, then the fact that the chef has sweated in the kitchen for four hours to produce some brilliant food is utterly ruined. It doesn't matter that the steak you've served the customer is the best they've ever eaten; they're not coming back.

Good food, value for money and good service are the backbone of the business. You want customers to be going out the door feeling they've had a good time and will come back. When they do come back it's important your staff recognise them and develop a customer relationship with them, get to know their names, and they become regular customers. Even visitors to Glasgow, which are now the bulk of our customers in the city centre, can become regulars as they'll make sure to come in whenever they're back in the city.

One of the biggest changes in terms of dining habits is the demise of the strict lunch and dinner settings. Before, people would come in for lunch only between 12 and say 1.30. You were dead for the rest of the afternoon so there was no point in staying open after 2. Then you would start serving from 5, or 5.30, sometimes as late as 6 and open for a few hours and close.

Now you could open at 11am and folk would be ordering three course meals. People come in all through the afternoon and right through the evening. You could be open 15 hours a day and customers would be in at either end. That traditional separation of lunch and dinner has gone.

The other key factor in maintaining success is stick to what you're good at. Don't try to do too much. If you do, you'll get lost, you'll dilute what you do best, and people won't know what you do.

For example, where our new West End restaurant is sited there's half-a-dozen coffee bars. But "coffee bars" is a bit misleading because they also sell soups, baguettes, paninis, toasties and so on. In other words, a wide range of foodstuffs. I'm not going to try and compete with that and start serving lattes with a biscuit. That caters to a different customer entirely. Two people in our restaurant paying £100 for dinner are not going to be too happy with hordes of people around them coming in and out and just having coffees and snacks. That's a different market. Some of the modern diners do try and do that, but not us. That's why I call us a "classic restaurant." The coffee bars are not competing with me and I've no intention of competing with them and everyone's happy.

Expanding west

We opened a second restaurant also called *La Lanterna* in the West End in the busy area of Kelvinbridge right on a major thoroughfare named Great Western Road. That opened in September 2017.

There are significant differences between customers at the two restaurants. A lot of hotels have opened in the city centre over the last five years which are close to the restaurant sited there. As a result, during the week, most of our customers are visitors, whether that be for business or for pleasure on short breaks. But because the restaurant's been there for so long, we have a substantial number of regular customers from across the city and further afield in Scotland, who have been coming for decades. In some cases, we're talking about families into the third generation.

By contrast, the West End restaurant is located in a residential area. About 70% of our customers in the West End are regulars, mainly families who live locally and 30% are visitors, whereas in the city centre it is the reverse. Most people coming into the West End restaurant walk there, which is certainly not true in the city-centre.

The average lifespan of a restaurant in Glasgow is probably about five years and we're long past that. There are only a few restaurants in Glasgow that have lasted as long as *La Lanterna* and you'll probably find most of those are family run. The reason for that is the commitment and dedication required. This is a lifestyle, a choice certainly, but a lifestyle nevertheless where you put in very long hours and sometimes weeks and months without a break.

The impetus to open a second restaurant was really curiosity. We knew it would it be fatal to try to recreate the city-centre restaurant as it is and transplant that to the West End. The city-centre restaurant is an institution. It's an old-established, Italian restaurant; its unique.

Our thinking for the new venue was: if we were opening a *La Lanterna* in 2017 what would it look like? What would people want and expect from it? The key is to give people what *they* want, not what *you* want. That's where a lot of restaurants go wrong. There are always room for improvements in any establishment but with the old restaurant it's a classic case of, if it's not broken don't try and mend it; you'll just drive people away. If I tried to convert the West End site into a copy of what the city-centre place is like, it would shut in about two weeks!

The city-centre site is a basement restaurant and I'm so glad because if it was on the ground on the first-floor people would see what goes on in the street outside. It's a very busy but anonymous non-residential area that's not very well lit and attracts a lot of unsavoury characters. And, unfortunately, the area has deteriorated further over the years, particularly during and after covid. So much so, I've had to put a controlled entry intercom system to secure it. It must be the only restaurant in Glasgow, if not Scotland, where customers need to press a buzzer to get in. People thought I was mad when I first installed it but believe me it's the best thing I've ever done, and it's not deterred customers.

Covid and after

Like everywhere else covid had a big impact on us. But it wasn't all bad. We opened a takeaway service in the West End and that has taken off. Because most of our customers are local, they're able to collect their orders and consume them at home quite soon after. I would say that takeaways easily pay for my electricity and gas at the West End restaurant.

Covid, or rather its aftermath, has had a particular impact on the city-centre site. That's because it has an older customer profile who were, for understandable reasons, quite nervous and cautious about coming back out as restrictions were lifting. It's only now, several years later, that nearly all those customers have come back, though we did lose some.

At the West End, we were only shut for about a total of eight weeks throughout the lockdown periods before we opened for takeaways and, as I said, that paid the bills. I own the premises in the city centre, and we did try takeaways there, but the city-centre was deserted, and it was a non-starter, so we just shut up shop.

It's true that, even though your premises were shut during lockdown and no income was coming in, you had no outgoings to pay and with the government paying your staff's wages through furlough, you could survive. But that only worked if you owned your premises and had no rent to pay. If you were renting and your landlord didn't give you a rent holiday, you were in a very precarious situation and many places had to shut for good. We were fortunate that way.

Nightclubbing at lunchtime

Back in 2000 Mike Tyson was in Glasgow for a boxing match. One of my regular customers in the city centre restaurant was a boxing promoter and he told me he was escorting the former UK heavyweight boxing champion, Frank Bruno, who'd become a TV pundit, from the airport as he was due to commentate on the match. The customer asked me if it would be ok if he brought Bruno into the restaurant. I said 'of course.'

The match was scheduled for Saturday evening, and this was Friday. About 6pm that night I received a phone call from the promoter who was at the airport with Frank Bruno. He asked me how busy the restaurant was, and I said it was almost full. He said he wasn't sure Frank would be 'happy' with that as he was recovering from some mental health issues. An hour later the promoter turns up and has a look around the restaurant. It's a typical bustling Friday evening. The promoter says: 'No, Frank wouldn't want to come in when it's like this.' I understood, so we made him food for Frank to eat in his hotel and he went away happy.

The next morning, as I was making my way to work, my phone rang; it was the promoter. He said to me: Frank loved the food we'd given him, and he would really love to have lunch at the restaurant. But could he have it exclusively for himself and his associates. I agreed and closed the restaurant to the public.

Frank turned up with about a dozen people and we had five staff catering for them between the restaurant and the kitchen. Meanwhile, upstairs, I've got staff at the entrance apologizing to people that we've had an "electrical fault" and were temporarily closed. As that's happening, Frank and his buddies have cranked our music system up full blast and are bopping like mad to Eminem's Slim Shady. They've turned the basement restaurant into a combination of a nightclub and a speakeasy in the bowels of Glasgow city centre at 1pm. Incredible! Mobile phones at that time were still quite basic with no cameras and there was no social media, so we had no way of recording it, which was a shame.

By this time, Frank Bruno was a very popular household celebrity appearing in adverts and quiz shows. He was a really, friendly guy. He took time to speak to all the staff, including the boys in the kitchen and everyone had a great time. I'll never forget when he shook my hands, his hands were huge, at least twice the size of mine. God help anybody on the receiving end of a punch from that guy!

We've had loads of other celebrities in over the years including actors such as Robert Duval, who was making a movie in Glasgow and Clint Eastwood as well as music stars, footballers and the like.

Advice

You need to be prepared to work long hours. If you're not prepared to do that then you have to depend on the people you've hired to work for you. The best thing you can do if you want to open a restaurant is to work at and know inside out every job going. If your chef walks out on you, which, thankfully, has never happened to me, you need to be prepared to work in that kitchen. You need to know how to cook every dish on your menu. The same with the cleaning and serving customers. Otherwise, you're dependent on other people and that, in this trade, is where it often goes badly wrong.

You also need people skills to deal with your customers. You need to understand and be able to look after people, make the place inviting for them.

The rewards are immense, not just financially from a successful restaurant and a good lifestyle but from meeting so many people from all walks of life. You're not cooped up in an office all day, But I must emphasise again, you need to work hard and commit to this.

Chris's favourite dish: Unashamedly, I'm going to say our lasagne we serve in our two restaurants and pasta fagioli which is pasta in bean soup. Thoroughly recommended.

Chris's favourite wine: Palazzo della Torre It's a mini Amarone from the famous Allegrini winery near Veneto.

17. PETER MCKENNA AND THE GANNET: HIGH END IN THE WEST END

From humble beginnings in Ireland, becoming personal chef to a Saudi Sheikh to running one of Glasgow's best-known high-end restaurants, and a good deal in between, Peter McKenna recounts his extraordinary story.

Beginnings

I was born in Monaghan town on the Republic side of the Irish border.

During the 80's the food scene in Ireland that I was aware of, left a lot to be desired.

I was fortunate growing up in a foodie household. Both my mother and grandmother were excellent cooks and cooked everything fresh from scratch. My mother lived in

London for many years and had an eclectic repertoire of dishes she liked to cook: Indian, Greek, Chinese, Italian as well as traditional Irish dishes. We were incredibly lucky.

Our family lived above my parents' pub and from an early age I was getting to grips with a life spent in hospitality, cleaning tables, collecting glasses, clearing out drip-trays and emptying ashtrays. When I was tall enough to look over the bar, I was pulling pints (though that was probably illegal). Those were the days when smoking was allowed in bars and my eyes would sting at the end of a shift.

I got to know the customers, a vibrant bunch, made up of music lovers from all walks of life.

Two of our regulars (soon to become dear friends) opened a Mediterranean restaurant a few doors down from the pub. I was fascinated by food, keen to learn how to cook restaurant style dishes, so cheekily asked if I could help out after school and at weekends.

They agreed and I learned to make a tremendous tiramisu and a whole host of other dishes. It was a lovely foundation and a good introduction to the industry.

Moving on I worked in a local hotel and after leaving school went to a culinary school in Donegal. During the course, we completed a few placements around Ireland, the most memorable was a castle in Kildare where I worked alongside my good friend Deano and the head chef was a young lad with a lot of talent.

The castle was beautiful with walled gardens which had a huge variety of herbs and vegetables. It was amazing to be around all this fresh produce. There is a massive difference in quality and taste between food just out of the ground and that which has been lying around on supermarket shelves for an age.

Going continental and down under

After completing my culinary course I was hungry for adventure, so along with a few close friends moved to

Holland where I ended up working in a meat processing plant for a few long weeks, that was a great catalyst for getting back into the kitchen. I managed to find a job working in a touristy restaurant under an Israeli chef who taught me quite a bit, we got on like a house on fire and he trusted me as a young cook to look after the meat and sauce section. I tried to get a position in a Michelin Starred restaurant but was initially turned down. However, with the help and encouragement of my chef I was eventually accepted.

I didn't know the language and had to pick it up while studying what they were cooking which was classic French cuisine. That gave me invaluable experience for when I moved to London.

I got a job in a restaurant called *Seven* working for Richard Turner who'd previously worked for Marco Pierre White for over 10 years at his peak.

I was only 20 and working in the kitchen with people of a very high calibre. There was loads of pressure - in fact there was nothing *but* pressure – but I kept my head down, worked all the hours and got on well with Richard. I was like a sponge learning whatever I could.

I spent a year in that kitchen before deciding to leave London and move to Australia. Before I left, Richard gave me two cookbooks. One was the *Banc Cookbook* by the esteemed chef Liam Tomlin and the *Est Est Est Cookbook* by another well-known chef Donavon Cook. He said to me: 'If you go to Sydney, you work *at Banc*, If you go to Melbourne, you work for *Est*.' There wasn't a job set up in either city but he gave me inspiration and direction.

When my great friend Marko and I arrived in Sydney we had very little money. We printed out CV's and together walked around the waterfront. Sydney Darling Harbour was awash with restaurants, and we handed CVs out everywhere. Remember this was long before Instagram and social media. You really needed books and guides to pinpoint where the good food was being cooked and I didn't even have a place to stay never mind a good food guide.

When we got to the Sydney Opera House, I saw it had a fine dining restaurant called the *Bennelong*, I thought to hell with it I'll brass neck it and see if I can chance a position. I walked in and left my CV at reception (young chefs please note all restaurants still like to get physical CVs handed in). As I was walking down the steps leaving the restaurant, I got a call from the head chef asking me back for a chat. We spoke briefly and he offered me a trial, I ended up working with them for three months as was allowed by my visa. The chef was brilliant, a great chap and had previously worked at 3-Star level in Paris.

After my time at the *Bennelong*, I planned to work in a ski resort. However, after a fateful tasting menu at *Banc* (I did listen to Richard), a meal I would describe as "transcendent" as it truly blew me away, I ended up staying in Sydney and joining Liam Tomlin and his team. My head chef, who had previously worked with Liam and knew him well, personally phoned him, and said to him 'this young Irish guy on a working holiday visa is in my kitchen and is ecstatic about your food, would you have a spot to offer him?' Liam told him to send me over for an interview, which I did, and he offered me a position. I was still swithering about the ski resort job, and I tried to negotiate, but Laim was having none of it and said: 'If you want to work here, you start on Friday or forget it.' So, all my grand plans for the ski job went out the window.

Liam sponsored me to extend my visa and helped me get temporary residency. But every day for the first three months in that kitchen I thought I was going to get sacked. I felt completely out of my depth. There'd been a lot of pressure at the other restaurants where I worked, but this was at a different level, extreme pressure. There was a revolving door of people who couldn't stand the pace. That year,

2001, *Banc* won the award for Australia's best restaurant and had 3 Chef Hats, the highest rating possible.

Just last week here at the *Gannet* one of the chefs I worked with back then came in for lunch. I hadn't seen him for 16 plus years. That was very special for me because that guy took me under his wing and that's how I survived. It was a great pleasure to be able to cook for him, I'd never had the opportunity before. We served him Grouse with wild mushrooms we'd foraged for ourselves, he loved it.

I met my wife, Chala, on a night out in Sydney. She was on a gap year before studying law at Glasgow University. After she left, we kept in touch by email. We became e-pen pals until meeting once again in Dublin.

Cooking at sea and on land for a Sheikh

When I finally finished up in Australia, I moved to Dublin and worked in the hotel owned by Bono and the Edge from U2 called the *Clarence*. The chef there was Anthony Eli. The world of fine dining is small, and Anthony knew a few of the people I'd worked with and known in Australia.

After Ireland I moved back to London and worked in *Chez Bruce*, a Michelin Star restaurant. That was a great restaurant but after receiving a call from a friend about joining a yacht in Germany my passion for adventure was sparked once again.

There'd been a head chef on board, but he'd left, and my friend was proposing he and I become joint head chefs. I'd no concept of what this meant, I thought it was some kind of sailing boat and we would cook for a handful of people.

I flew to the port in Germany where the "yacht" was in a dry dock. When I saw this massive yacht (72 meters) it was more like a ship than a yacht. It was in fact a private motor yacht; owned by a prominent Saudi Sheikh. The kitchen was larger than the one in *Chez Bruce* and they offered me a job on the spot which I couldn't refuse. I worked my notice in London and moved out to join the crew.

Being a chef on board a motor yacht is a whole new way of doing things. As well as cooking you're basically in charge of logistics for provisioning food for the ship, organising the fridge and a myriad of other tasks which are specific to cooking on board a ship at sea. I learnt a whole new skillset and got on well with the captain and the entourage. In fact, after a year in the company whenever the boss wasn't on board, we flew on a private plane to places like the Seychelles, Beirut and Saudi.

I had to cook on the private jet, as well. It's a different world on board a private plane. There's no sitting with seat belts on while the plane is taking off. People were walking up and down speaking on their mobiles while I'm getting the kitchen fired up as the plane's taking off and almost vertical! That lasted for four years, and I experienced a taste of a jet set lifestyle, even if I was just the hired help.

There was a memorable incident while I was at the palace in Jeddah. My boss loved sea food especially sea bass and tuna. The problem was the waters around Saudi are murky and warm and the fish in those seas weren't to the Bosses taste. One day, the suppliers to the palace, who also supply the Saudi King, arrived with all these containers of fish, none of which I thought were suitable. After I rejected all of them, the supplier was raging, saying: 'how dare you, I supply the King!'

Now I was 24, young and a bit reckless, so I just said back to him: 'I don't care who you supply, I'm not giving this to my boss!'

That's not something you really say to a supplier to the King in a country like Saudi. He was a well-respected man and I got into a wee bit of trouble, but the boss's right-hand man bailed me out. He booked a private jet for the two of us to Geneva where we stayed at the 5-star *Presidente Hotel*. We spent a day there lugging these empty chill boxes around all the best shops selling seafood and loaded up with the finest fish and shellfish. We flew back the next day with the fish. I worked through the night preparing and freezing the haul.

So, there's me, a wee lad from Monaghan, telling off suppliers to royalty and jet setting between palaces and 5-star hotels on shopping expeditions. Unbelievable!

Coming to Glasgow and opening the *Gannet*

After four years of this way of working on yachts and in palaces, I needed to get back into the 'normal' restaurant business worried that I may have lost my touch. I moved to Glasgow, bought a house with my girlfriend, and worked under Craig Dunn at *Michael Caines @ Abode* in the city centre as a *chef de partie* on the sauce section. Within a few months I was promoted to sous chef. That boosted my confidence greatly and I got on like a house on fire with Craig.

I worked at *Abode* for several years and while there met my business partner, Ivan Stein, where we worked on the idea to open our own place which would eventually be the *Gannet*. You can hatch a plan in your head overnight, but it takes years to come to fruition or it did in our case. We looked at many sites across the city, though we always gravitated towards the West End. The problem was nothing suitable came onto the market. Places that might have suited us were being bought and sold between people that knew each other. I didn't have any reputation so wasn't in the loop.

Eventually, it was John McLeod at *Crabshack* who put us onto a vacant site that was about to come onto the market near his own restaurant in Finneston. It was derelict with no services at all. The front was boarded up and had been like that for years. All told, it took years to negotiate the lease, transform the site and turn it into a restaurant. During that time, I often wondered, is this ever going to happen? I even considered moving back to Australia. However, I did get offered a job as head chef on a Russian oligarch's yacht, a great move where I met some truly inspiring people and another business partner and great friend Peter Read.

This position pushed me outside my comfort zone, and I acquired considerable experience in becoming resilient.

New to social media I used it to document the work on the site. I noticed that some prominent food critics were interested and following the transformation as it unfolded. We visited farms and worked on developing supply chains because our concept was of a "farm-to-table" restaurant. Those connections and networks take years to really develop, but we got there in the end.

I wanted to have a place that would take the best from the Scottish larder: game, wild mushroom, seafood and offer that to the guests, a simple plan. I would carry out all the butchery and sauce work and the menu would be made up of the type of food and dishes we gravitated towards.

After all our planning and extensive coverage on social media, we opened. For us it was a big deal, but for other people it's just another bloody restaurant!

The first couple of years were difficult because nobody seemed to know what we were about. Ivan, my business partner, even contemplated changing the concept but I resisted. There were great reviews from critics, and you think after a good review, the place should be mobbed, but it wasn't. It took time to gather pace.

There were loads of challenges. We had power cuts at peak times over the weekends. Not being able to afford losing customers we cooked food by candlelight over a barbecue! We got through it with smiles all round from our very accommodating guests. There were many difficult nights. But despite all that, the *Gannet* became a great success.

After a year of trading, we were very lucky to be joined by Kevin Dow who took over the front of house operations and made it his own, a likeminded sole passionate about the wild larder and the endless possibilities it holds both medicinal and gastronomical.

We've been going for over ten years now and we're on the culinary map which is incredibly satisfying.

Just recently, we held a celebration in the restaurant for some of the people that worked at the restaurant throughout the years including friends, and suppliers. It was amazing to hear how people held their time with us in such high regard. That's the amazing thing about this trade, you can come from anywhere and be a success, it's a great leveller and if you put in the hard work and dedication, you can achieve great things.

Advice

For the first few years, keep your head down, absorb everything because those first years will stand you for the rest of your time in the industry. Work in good restaurants with high standards under chefs who know what the hell they're doing. Work the hours, do the time. Learn the recipes, write them down, don't just follow them, think about what you're doing and why.

It's an industry that if you want to excel in it you have to immerse yourself in it, live and breathe it, it's not nine-to-five and do not ever expect it to be.

Peter's favourite dish: My mother used to make a traditional roast beef but with beautiful homemade onion bhajis on the side, that's not traditional, I grant you, but it worked.

Peter's favourite wine: I grew up in a pub in Ireland, so it wouldn't be a wine, it would be a pint of Guiness. But if pushed a nice Gevrey Chambertin always hits the spot.

18. ZOLTAN SZABO: THE MASTER CRAFTSMAN OF FOOD

From his background in Hungary, Zoltan Szabo has carved a distinctive reputation in a variety of high-end venues in Scotland. Now after a period of overseeing a good quality farm shop selling the finest artisan Scottish produce, Zoltan is the Executive Head Chef at the quality Hazel Restaurant by the AC Marriot Hotel in Glasgow. Here, he retraces his culinary journey.

Beginnings

I was born in the southern part of Hungary in the early 1980s. No-one in my family worked in hospitality or catering. My father and grandfather worked as miners. Hungary was then part of the old Eastern Block, allied to the Soviet Union.

Back in the Soviet era if you performed long service in the coal mines you could retire early. Depending on the length of service you worked as a miner, you would be awarded a small holding, essentially a small farm. In my grandfather's case this was approximately 50 acres of land.

I was mostly brought up on my grandfather's land surrounded by livestock, mainly a breed of pigs called Mangalitsa and other large white pigs, a few sheep, farmed rabbits as well as various poultry from free range ducks and geese through to chickens. We also pressed grapes and made our own wine and grew most of our own vegetables and fruits. I remember we would preserve our carrots by layering them between sand in a purpose-built wooden bench in the cellar.

Our livestock was slaughtered by my family, and we made our own smoked and air-dried hams and salamis which were flavoured by paprika made by my grandfather's sister's family. My mother also made her own jams and sauerkraut. So, I was raised in a self-sufficient way around farm animals and cooking and eating good, fresh food.

I was 14 when I had to choose a trade. I had two options in mind; either to become a stonemason or a chef. I reckoned that I would always have work as a stonemason as there would be a constant demand from rich people for gravestones made from good quality Italian marble. But then I figured those same rich people would always want good quality food prepared by chefs and I could live off the breadcrumbs left by them. So why spend the rest of my life lifting heavy marble stones when I could become a chef?

Learning the trade

I went to catering college for four years. While there, I worked in a local restaurant at night and at weekends. I also pursued a self-taught hobby of carving vegetables into the shapes of swans or roses which I'd make from the likes of carrots. I won a few competitions for this. This hobby proved very useful for me when I moved to Budapest, the capital, in 2002. I was 160 miles from home and had £20 worth of Hungarian forints in my pocket, but through force of personality and with the help of friends I was able to find accommodation and get by. Then, through a stroke of good fortune, my vegetable carving hobby gave me the first step on the ladder to becoming a chef.

There was a TV show about catering which also featured food themed contests. I entered my vegetable carvings for one of these contests and won. The host of the TV show was Gianni Annoni who was also the owner of one of Hungary's best Italian restaurants, *Trattoria Pomo D'oro*. He was so impressed by my winning entry that he offered me a full-time position in his trattoria where I worked for two years. I have sweet memories of my time working with Gianni and his team. Their passion for food was contagious and this is where I learned to make fresh pasta, breads and to appreciate the ingredients for what they are.

While there I still carved vegetables and fruits for hotels to use on their buffet displays. One of these hotels was the iconic *Inter-Continental Budapest*, which was located on the banks of the Danube. That was also fortuitous, because I met Hungary's best ice carver, Zsolt M Toth who would take blocks of ice and make wonderful carvings from them. I was very keen to learn how to do this and arranged to visit his apartment and see how it was done. While I was there one day, he received a phone call from a contact of his in Finland who owned a restaurant and was looking for a chef. Zsolt recommended me. I jumped at the opportunity and within a month I was ready to leave Hungary.

Going international

I had no command of Finnish, German or English at the time. I learned by the staff showing me an object like a spoon and saying the name in both Finnish and English. I would then write it down on a paper and memorise it. After a week most objects in the kitchen would have a sticker on them displaying their names. By this means, over the two years I was in Finland, I managed to pick up the elementary English that would allow me to communicate better and travel further. After two years working in Finland, I went back home.

There I came across an advert in a newspaper for Hilton Hotels International who were recruiting chefs. I applied and was interviewed in Budapest. Everybody else's interview lasted for 15-20 minutes, mine was for over an hour. I brought along pictures and presentations of the food I was experienced in cooking and preparing and basically "entertained" the interview panel. By the time I arrived back at my parent's home I'd received an email offering me a job at a Hilton Hotel in Glasgow in the UK.

Carving a name in Scotland.

I flew to Newcastle, and due to my late arriving flight, I missed the train to Glasgow and spent my first night in the UK sleeping in Newcastle railway station before catching a train next morning to Glasgow. That was Halloween 2005.

My first job in Scotland was as a *chef de partie* at the *Hilton Glasgow* on William Street in Glasgow under the Executive Chef James Murphy. I learnt a lot from Chef Murphy and worked my way up the ladder.

Within a few months of starting at the *Hilton*, I was put in charge of the fine dining restaurant which was called *Camerons*. It was an amazing experience working there as I was able to work with so many new ingredients and styles. I left *Hilton* Glasgow in 2007 and went to work for the *McDonald Hotel* at Aberfoyle in Perthshire. After just four months I was promoted into the Head Chef role by the General Manager of the hotel, Allan Reich. I can never be grateful enough for Allan's confidence and trust in me and I worked there until the end of 2009.

Then in 2010 I was reunited with Chef Murphy for the opening of the New *Grand Central Hotel* at Glasgow Central Station. This hotel was a famous establishment in the city. A former restaurant at the hotel, the *Malmaison* (not to be confused with the current hotel of that name in the city) was legendary as a fine dining establishment in Glasgow long before that term was in wide use. That places a special responsibility on you to maintain that reputation and tradition, and we were determined to do so.

Chef Murphy and I got access to the building before it opened. That was important because we were able to work with the architects and contractors to design the kitchen layout to what we wanted. I remember how we would go round the site with hard hats, hi-vis jackets, steel boots, and torches with rolled up plans. Chef Murphy knew the building inside out as he'd began working as a commis chef at the old *Central Hotel* in the early 1980s, just a few years before I was born!

Theatrical dining

I moved on from there to work at *Cameron House* on the shores of Loch Lomond for about ten months before I received a pleasant phone call asking if I would like to be the Executive Head Chef at the *Blythswood Square Hotel*, a 5-star, 50 bed, boutique hotel in the heart of Glasgow with an accompanying spa. I jumped at the opportunity.

I had the chance to try out innovative dishes with new ingredients and improve the private dining and afternoon tea offerings alongside Chef Gillian Eagleson (who went onto become Executive Chef for the hotel after my departure in 2019).

I love bringing theatrical elements into the service such as opening Orkney scallops baked in the shells for guests, hosting interactive truffle dinners, grating parmesan at the table, or carving while roasted monkfish tale at the table side.

My team at the *Blythswood Square Hotel* embraced it wholeheartedly. We had the opportunity to host private dining evenings such as truffle and game nights, Moet & Chandon events and so on.

I clearly remember the night we held a truffle event with a table set for 20 people. In the middle of this table there were tree leaves, barks, logs, and little containers of soil, all aesthetically pleasing. There were also different sizes and colours of pumpkins, quince and herbs. We carefully placed canapes amongst these which the guests could pick out for themselves.

We brought out the first course which was my all-time favourite Orkney scallops with chestnut agnolotti that was sauced table side. After the first course, we asked the diners to forage through the "forest" on the table to find a truffle and the person who found it won a dinner for two complete with wine at the hotel. The excitement, buzz and happiness that generated among the guests was incredible. These are the moments I love seeing and makes everything worthwhile. The next course was a quail dish followed by a red deer Wellington. The dinner was concluded with a serving of dessert that was made using mushrooms. Yes, you read that right, *mushrooms*. The dessert has a story of its own.

When I was a child, I used to go mushroom picking with my grandfather and his favourite mushroom was cep. I cherished those moments and now I take my own two children mushroom picking whenever they are in season. Because of this I love mushrooms and I would put them in everything, even desserts. My inspiration for this stemmed from when I once dined in London at a restaurant called *Hibiscus* where the kitchen was headed by a world-famous chef called Claude Bossi. There was this sensational dessert of cep tartlet served with macadamia nut ice cream. After I finished my meal, I had a tour of the kitchen and was cheeky enough to ask the recipe for the tartlet. I didn't just get the dish verbally explained to me but was given the recipe. I felt so humbled that such a prestigious establishment would do that!

Dining in the sky

While at the *Blythswood Square* Hotel, I had the opportunity to cook for the opening ceremony as well as numerous other lunch and early dinner settings at a festival called Events in The Sky. We cooked and served food in a 90-foot giant crane hoisted above George Square, right in the centre of Glasgow. We served about 12-to-15 people per sitting. Their napkins were secured so they could not fly away. I cooked at this aerial festival with my private dining head chef at the *Blythswood*, Derek Blair, a fantastic chef who is very well respected in the industry. Our only cooking facilities were a small induction type of stove and a tiny oven. The crane was lowered once to allow the dessert ingredients on board, and we would carry on cooking. It was an amazing experience which the guests loved. There are not many chefs who can say they've cooked food 90 feet up on a crane above a major city square!

After several years at the *Blythswood Square Hotel,* I went back to the *Grand Central Hotel* and was delighted to see that many of the team I'd started there with when it re-opened were still together and had really developed and transformed the venue over that time; testament to Chef Murphy.

Mentoring future talent

In the autumn of 2019, I was invited to judge the Springboard Future Chef competition at the City of Glasgow College. The winner was a 15-year-old schoolgirl called Jodie Cochrane. I then had the chance to mentor Jodie in the kitchen of the *Grand Central Hotel* and provide her with more techniques ahead of the next heat of the competition in January 2020. She was really dedicated and gave up her evenings after school and weekends to work with me. That paid off and Jodie won the next heat and went on to represent Scotland at the UK national finals in London. She progressed to win the Springboard Future Chef of the Year title against fierce competition.

For me this was the most cherished moment of my career to date. To have mentored Jodie and to watch her develop and then compete and win at these levels was a privilege and a great reward. This one goes out to Jodie. Her dedication and commitment have inspired me and many other Springboard Future Chefs too since she won the title. That's a proud legacy to have.

Lockdown: The world stops as we know it.

Two weeks after Jodie won that competition we went into lockdown and the world stopped as we know it. Lockdown occurred two weeks before I was due to begin work at *Cameron House*. As I've mentioned, I'd worked there before but now I was going back as Executive Head Chef.

Way back in 2005 when I first came to Scotland, I remember taking a walk along the shores of Loch Lomond and coming across the magnificent building that is Cameron House and thinking to myself how I would love to work there, never believing that 15 years later I would have the privilege of reopening the hotel.

I started in April of 2020 reporting to the Resource Director, Andy Roger who is the most inspiring manager I've ever worked with. Andy's attention to detail is impeccable and he is more focused on the customer journey than any other director or general manager I've ever worked with.

We reopened this very prestigious and internationally renowned hotel in the early autumn of 2021 after most covid restrictions had been lifted. I felt just as lucky to be part of it as little Charlie Bucket was when he found the Golden Ticket in Willy Wonka's chocolate bar. A few weeks after re-opening we had the COPT 26 environmental conference in Glasgow, and we hosted a number of world leaders as well as celebrities and the former President of the United States,

Barack Obama. These were exciting events and it's always a great experience to cater for high-profile people.

Having said that, it is much more satisfying to cater for everyday people. The rich and powerful can always afford luxury hotels and fine dining. It's not a novelty to them. In contrast, when you're charging between £250 - £2500 per room for one night's accommodation, everyday people have to save for months for that. Invariably, they're staying with you for a special celebration which they're looking forward to so much. You as the chef along with the hotel's management teams, the waiters, the front-of-house staff, all have a duty of care to ensure that their experience is special from the moment they arrive until they depart.

For example, at *Cameron House* we worked hard to make the children's afternoon tea experiences very special and magical. Before it was a hotel, *Cameron House* was a bear park and the first bear to be born there was named Patrick. We devised an afternoon tea for children where on arrival, they would find a wooden pattern box on the dining table with a luxurious soft teddy bear warring different colours of knitted jumper sitting next to it. When they opened it, they would find little sweets and savoury treats and a scroll addressed to them. The scroll would be from "Patrick" explaining he'd already had some treats on his way from the magical Cameron House Fairy Trail and had thought to "order" a selection of playful treats for the child as well.

I can remember watching the first service and seeing the look of surprise and delight on the child's face and that of their parents.

All this was to create an unforgettable experience for them that they will always associate with the hotel and cherish for years to come.

Down on the farm

In the summer of 2022, I moved onto a new venture called *Barnhill Farm* near Glasgow Airport, a 70-acre farm owned by James Mackie. Farm shops are usually passed down through the generations, but *Barnhill Farm* only opened recently. James's dedication to the local community and to grow the farm shop is amazing. It's more than a farm shop though. The farm has twenty herd of Highland cattle, a flock of Hebridean sheep, Clydesdale horses and Mangalitsa pigs. There's also a wild cross-boar called Medlar which was used to cross with the pigs to breed what is called Iron-Age pigs. That's the name given to the offspring of wild boars crossed with domestic pigs.

It also has an in-house butchery department which uses the farm's cattle, sheep and pigs and also sources local milk available only 20 minutes' drive from the farm shop and which tastes a lot richer and creamier than those sold in supermarkets. As there's always fresh local milk available, the farm decided to build a gelato room which can make 25 litres of gelato in an hour.

As a farm shop they always have an abundance of fresh fruit and vegetables which are sold to customers and also wholesale to hotels and restaurants in and around Glasgow.

Jams and sauces are made to their own specifications, and they produce seasonal compotes too. Absolutely everything on the farm is fresh and made in-house which means there's total control of the items they sell.

The farm was a great success for me. Coming from a smallholding and butchery background to be able to work with what you breed is tremendous. With the farm I felt as if I'd gone back to my beginnings but in my new country.

After a successful stint at *Barnholl* I'm now working at the *Hazel Restaurant* part of the AC Marriot Hotel back in Glasgow city centre.

Advice

Absorb everything you see. Always have a pen and notebook with you and note everything. Above all, you must have a positive attitude. You can always learn the skills required. It is much more difficult to keep a polite and positive attitude, but with the right approach and commitment you can go very far.

Zoltan's favourite dish: I could not pinpoint one single dish, however, coming from a farming background, home cured and smoked charcuterie and foie gras run through my veins.

Zoltan's favourite wine: A nice red Zinfandel or lovely Barolo or Bordeaux.

19. TREVOR LEE & OPIUM: BRINGING ASIAN FUSION FOOD TO THE DEAR GREEN PLACE

Trevor Lee opened Opium in Glasgow in 2010. Since then, the restaurant has made a great contribution to the Glasgow dining experience with its distinctive blend of Asian fusion cuisine. Trevor explains the challenges and joys of bringing opium to the people.

Beginnings

My journey in the hospitality and restaurant business began in 1973, when a three-course lunch was merely 48 pence. As immigrants from Hong Kong to the UK, our initial challenges were predominantly linguistic. The restaurant industry promised a setting where language was secondary to the universal love for food and service. I started my career working in restaurants in Manchester where I gradually cultivated the skills necessary to work in cuisine and acquired a deep-seated passion for the business.

One of the restaurant owners I worked with recognised both my enthusiasm and potential and provided me with support and guidance. At the same time, I was really attracted to working in the kitchen with its symphony of flavours and aromas. My older brother had extensive experience of working in a kitchen and, on my days off, I would join him there learning how a kitchen works and cultivating my love of cuisine. For me, these weren't just workplaces, they were more like classrooms.

This restaurant owner's father was a maestro at the art of preparing, cooking, and serving dim sum, and with his guidance, I gleaned invaluable insights into this delicate art. By stringing pieces of the language together I gradually improved my English and my confidence at working in the restaurant industry.

Before *Opium*, I worked in various establishments of which *Yang Sing* in Manchester was probably the most significant. I spent a very fruitful year there learning so much in a very busy, high pressured, bustling environment. After working there for a few years, I took up the manager's position at another busy restaurant in Manchester called *Kai*, where I worked for four years. The chef in *Kai* was also the owner. He was a culinary expert, a master of his craft who had been working in kitchens since he was eight!

As the owner's father approached his 70s, I gave up the manager's role, put on the chef's whites and took over from him in the kitchen.

Coming to Glasgow

I came to Glasgow in 1979, when my brother, who ran a small dim sum venue in the city, was needing some help. I found a city that was vibrant and buzzing with wonderful architecture. But as they say, it was the people of Glasgow who made it special. They were open and genuine and made me feel welcome, easing my transition into this new city. Quite quickly, Glasgow became for me not just a city but a canvas, inviting and inspiring at the same time. I've stayed ever since and made myself at home here.

From my brother's venue I moved on to manage a restaurant in Sauchiehall Street called the *New City Palace* which, again, was very busy and popular, located right in the heart of Glasgow's nightlife area. It had its challenges and opportunities and provided me with more experience and allowed me to become even more familiar with the unique personality of the city. Unfortunately, a fire broke out in the premises and the place closed. But it gave me the confidence of opening my own restaurant which became *Opium*.

Giving *Opium* to the people

I opened *Opium* in 2010 on the site of what had been a very popular Chinese Restaurant called *Peking Inn* which was in the city centre. The atmosphere, style of restaurant and the food I wanted to serve were very different from the previous restaurant. I wanted to have a calmer ambience and low-lit background than is usual for Chinese restaurants. The menu was and still is a fusion of Chinese, Malaysian and Thai cuisine.

Opium is NOT a place which will serve chow mein or chop suey. There is nothing wrong with those dishes, but you can get them anywhere. I wanted to serve something different and original, though we do serve traditional dim sum.

I wasn't sure how this would go down in Glasgow.

What a difference a review makes

For the first nine months, after our grand opening in 2010, we were quiet. I thought I'd made a terrible mistake with the restaurant. Each day rolled into the next with few customers. Then, one Sunday, without warning, the restaurant filled with customers. Halfway through the afternoon one of our regular customers produced a newspaper and directed my attention to a review. It was of our restaurant. I'd no idea it was going into the newspaper.

Nervously, I read the review. As I perused It, I relaxed. The review was glowing. It was by Joanna Blythman, one of Scotland's best-known food critics. She gave us a ten-out-of-ten rating and this provided the restaurant with a tremendous boost.

When I saw her picture at the top of the review, I suddenly remembered the lady. She had come into the restaurant a few weeks earlier, though I'd no idea at the time who she was. I recalled how she'd shown a keen interest in our menu. She asked detailed questions and her enjoyment. was evident as she savoured each dish. Her review reflected the keen interest and appreciation she'd displayed about our food. That review was a tremendous compliment to the effort we put into every dish and our commitment to good service.

It's fair to say we owe a lot to that one review. It brought them in that Sunday, and they've kept coming since. I think it's no exaggeration to say that *Opium* is consistently one of the most popular Chinese restaurants in the city and that's testimony to the high standards we continuously strive to maintain.

Challenges

One constant challenge we face is persistent staff shortages. For example, recruiting chefs, who are the backbone of any restaurant, has grown increasingly difficult. This is a demanding profession requiring long unconventional hours and dedication. I do believe that the lure of tech jobs and careers with more sociable hours has siphoned talent away from our vibrant but tough and exacting field.

However, these challenges, which are common to all restaurants irrespective of the kind of food they serve, has not dampened our resolve at *Opium* to serve our customers exquisite meals that offer more than just flavours but an experience.

Advice

It is vital for anyone considering opening a restaurant to invest in long-term, committed staff. Having a reliable and dedicated team in place is invaluable. Your staff are not just employees; they are the face of your restaurant, the individuals who will carry your vision and interact with the customers daily. They need to share your commitment to providing exceptional service and be willing to grow and adapt as the restaurant evolves. That means *you* – whether you are the owner or manager – must foster an environment where staff feel valued and supported. That will encourage them to stay for the long term in an industry noted for its high turnover of staff.

Long-term staff bring consistency and familiarity, which enhances the dining experience for repeat customers.

Your staff's understanding of the restaurant's principles and operations also contributes significantly to a smoother operation. It's essential not only to hire skilled individuals but to cultivate a sense of belonging and loyalty among your team. Ensure you offer opportunities for professional development, and create a positive, inclusive workplace culture. Remember, a restaurant that is supported by a strong, cohesive team is well on its way to establishing itself as a reputable and beloved establishment in the community.

Trevor's favourite dish(s): Dim Sum, with Crab & Chive Dumplings holds a special place for me. Each dumpling is a delightful bite of tender crab meat, perfectly seasoned with fresh chives, offering a burst of flavour that's both subtle and captivating.

I also have a fondness for Char Siu, where the roasting process unveils a sweet and tender symphony of pork that is simply hard to resist.

Then there's exquisite Langoustine, delicately blanched and adorned with slivers of ginger and spring onion, offering a taste that's both delicate and deeply satisfying.

Trevor's favourite wine: My go-to white wine is the Gruner Veltliner from Austria, an amazing companion to a variety of dishes with its crisp, refreshing notes and subtle complexity. My favourite red wine is Chateau Minvielle Bordeaux Superieur, a personal favourite.

20. STEPHEN CRAWFORD: REGIONAL HEAD CHEF WITH SIX BY NICO; COMMITMENT, RESILIENCE & TALENT

From kitchen porter to becoming executive head chef for one of Scotland's most famous chefs, Stephen Crawford has enjoyed a momentous career. Here, he candidly recalls the pitfalls and the milestones on the way to that success.

Beginnings

I was born in Largs, a small resort town on the Clyde coast about 20 miles outside Glasgow. From the age of 14 I worked as a kitchen porter (KP) in restaurants and when I left school at 16 worked at *Nardini's* a famous ice cream parlour in Largs.

There were three sections: a café, the ice cream parlour, and a restaurant. I worked in the café and served soups and sandwiches and how to organise and clean until I worked my way up to the main kitchen.

There I cooked starters and mains and learned the basics. A new head chef, Chris Rouse, took me under his wing and from him I learned how to cook steaks, fish, pasta and so on. I really started to enjoy it. I was 17 and I thought I can really do this; it's what I want to do.

In addition, I started to enjoy the food and flavours I'd never had before such as, for example, king prawns. My family were bland eaters, and this was an entirely different experience. While at *Nardini's* I did a college-on-site course in the kitchen. The lecturer was a guy called Alasdair McCallum, a local man, who'd been head chef at the Turnberry Golf Course. He encouraged me to go up to the next level and I started searching around.

Too much too soon: Moving to the world of fine dining.

On my eighteenth birthday I did a trial shift at the world-famous *Gleneagles Hotel* in Perthshire and was accepted. It was a huge change from Largs, and I was away from home for the first time, and I lived in digs at the hotel. I stayed at *Gleneagles* for three years and left just after my twenty first birthday.

During my time at Gleneagles, I moved onto the main kitchen of the *Strathearn Restaurant* which had a 2 Rosettes award. This was a mark of quality from the AA, not quite the same as a Michelin Star but a good badge to have. I started again at the bottom in the kitchen and found the first months there hard going. There were older chefs and I was trying to keep up. I felt I wasn't getting anywhere, that I was going backwards.

Then, one night, I moved onto the grill cooking steaks and I had a great night, my confidence was boosted, and I felt I was on top of it once more. A lot of times all I've needed is that little boost and belief in myself. After that I started pushing for new things on the menu. Once you start to earn the respect of the chefs around you it becomes much better. A lot of the times you're not only working closely with your fellow chefs but staying with them as well in shared accommodation, so you become friends.

After three years at Gleneagles, a couple of the chefs I knew, Mark Donald and Ian Scaramuza, went down to work in the kitchens at Claude Bosi's Two Star Michelin restaurant in London's Mayfair called *Hibiscus*. At their invitation I went down and did a week's free trial. I really enjoyed it. It was another step up, the pressure was enormous, and you were doing 17–18-hour days but I took to it. A few months later I went down for another free trial to show how keen I was, and they offered me a position. That was in 2013.

But it was a step too far for me. Although both the *Gleneagles* and the *Strathearn* were fine dining establishments, *Hibiscus* was on a different level entirely. The pressure was unrelenting, and you were doing 80–90-hour weeks. The money wasn't great either, which made it harder to enjoy my time in London.

I'm not shy in admitting this, but I felt out of my depth. I had a good long chat to myself and with my family and my fellow chefs (because I didn't want to let them down). Eventually, after six months, I conceded defeat and handed my notice in. When I look back on it, I can see that sometimes you can push through barriers, other times you can't and there's no point in kidding yourself. A lot of the chefs I worked with in London are now Michelin Star status and working in places like San Francesco and Berlin, but that wasn't to be for me. I had to take a different path.

Getting back on the horse

I picked myself up and with the help of Mark the sous chef I obtained a position at *Cail Brui*ch, a traditional Scottish restaurant in the West End of Glasgow., in January 2014. It was there that I learned the core of my cooking and skills set. They had 2 Rosettes at the time, and I learned recipes and systems. Above all they served a really good standard of food with a lot of variation from lunch to dinner menus and the tasting menu which gave me a wide range of experience.

I worked at *Cail Bruich* for 18 months and then I got an offer to work again with Chris Rouse, who I'd worked with at *Nardini's*. He had opened a new restaurant on the Southside of Glasgow called *Black Dove*. I took him up on the opportunity. It was a good restaurant in many ways and got a lot of decent reviews. Sadly, the restaurant didn't last long, about three years and if I'm honest, looking back on it, I was still quite inexperienced. But I feel experiences like this help in the long run.

Moving onto Nico's and the madness of lockdown

While at *Black Dove* I received a call from a guy named Nico who'd opened a restaurant called *Six by Nico* at Finneston in the West End. He invited me in a for a chat, said he'd heard a lot about me and offered me a trial shift. I liked the place and what Nico was doing. I left *Black Dove* and very quickly took to working in *Six by Nico*. I was still only 24 with loads to learn in this game, and I felt comfortable and on top of things in my new position.

On my first day there, I was working under this chef who was a chef at Nico's other restaurant in Glasgow, *111*. He was at *Six* for a few weeks until I took over and then he was going to work at Nico's father-in-law's restaurant. So, on that first day I was chatting to the chef, getting to know him. We were both in similar positions financially with debts to pay and general money worries. While we were prepping away, he suddenly turned to me and said: 'mate, I think I've won a million pounds.'

I thought he'd lost the plot or had received one of those dodgy emails, but, no, his numbers had come up on the Millionaire Draw on the National Lottery. He had to phone to confirm and came back declaring he had won a million quid. He was quite chirpy but a bit underwhelmed; I think I was more ecstatic than he was. Believe it or not he stayed on to work his final two weeks' notice. On his last night, we all went on a celebratory night out with him and ended up going to the casino. But he still behaved as if he'd just won a few hundred quid instead of a million. He didn't splash out and I ended up buying more rounds of drinks than he did! However, I can say that I'm one of the few people who's known and worked beside a lottery winner.

I worked for four-and-a-half years at *Six by Nico* and helped to open a new restaurant for them in Edinburgh which was a great experience and, again, greatly helped my confidence as I now felt, 'hi, I'm a guy that helps to open restaurants.'

I became head chef in what is a very systems-based operation. There are six set items on the menu, and they're changed religiously every six weeks (thus Six by Nico) and you get a great chance to learn new recipes and new ways of working. All told, I really enjoyed working there. And then came covid.

At first a lot of chefs thought "sorted", we'll get some time off because everybody believed it would only last a couple of weeks. A year later places were still closed or very limited to when they could open. It was traumatic. Places are still failing to this day. There is a massive hangover lingering from covid which is still going on.

I was working in Edinburgh *Nico's* at the time, and we had to adapt and came up with the idea of a home delivery service called Home by Nico which I prepared in the kitchen and then drove around Edinburgh in a van delivering to customers. Remember it was a pandemic, not some inconvenience such as a gas leak or a flooding which had caused you to close for a short period. This was a full-blown epidemic and you had to keep safe and secure.

It was funny how in a busy restaurant chefs can dream of time off, but when you're faced with a prolonged shutdown or working almost alone in a kitchen, you really do miss the teamwork and the buzz of a bustling restaurant. We came through it though and we were glad to get back to normality.

Even before covid I was thinking of moving on and had planned to move to Australia in 2020 with my fiancée, Jessie, one of the managers at Nico's. We'd obtained visas and booked our flights but covid scuppered that and we thought maybe the overseas' venture is not to be and best stay put here.

After the first lockdown was lifted, we still had restrictions in place. So, for example, the covers at *Six by Nico* were reduced from 40 to 20. At this stage Nico's were expanding throughout the UK and Nico himself offered me the post of Executive Head Chef with a brief to go across all the Nico sites. It involved travelling after being cooped up during lockdown. It was also a promotion with better money, and I would be working with more teams, so I was happy to take up the opportunity.

My new position didn't start well. The first new restaurant on my watch was in Manchester on the first day of Eat Out to Help Out, which was a government scheme to help hospitality recover from lockdown by paying them to discount their prices and attract customers to come back out. As a result, the restaurant was incredibly busy and to be frank, the chefs were not the best. We were serving a six-course tasting menu with 300 covers per day while still in semi lock down. It wasn't easy. But this time I got through the barrier, and we got on top of it, not least by finding better staff.

I did that role for a year, and I enjoyed it, but it took its toll. You were constantly travelling around the country, staying in hotels, working up to 90 hours per week and on your day off, you often spent four or five hours on a train back to Glasgow before you were back out the next day.

I decided it was time to move on, but I left *Nico's* amicably. I helped to prepare the last six-item menu for them (as I said, the menu changes every six weeks) and they were happy with that. Indeed, my partner still works in recruitment for *Six by Nico's*.

Working with Nick Nairn

From *Nico* I went to work for hotel owner and chef Tom Lewis who owned *Monachyle Mhor* which is a boutique hotel with a restaurant situated in a beautiful, secluded setting on a loch near the village of Lochearnhead. Tom and his family had their own butchery, farm and bakery which supplied fresh produce to the hotel. I was working as a sous chef for the first time alongside head chef Marysia. At the age of 22 I'd went from *chef de partie* to head chef and then executive head chef and missed out sous chef. After the stresses and strains of the last few years I just wanted to go back to cooking food. I wanted to love it again which I felt I hadn't the past few years.

I enjoyed working at *Monachyle Mhor* even though the travelling back and forth to Glasgow was tiring. The food was excellent, and I enjoyed cooking it. One of the owner's friends was Nick Nairn, probably one of Scotland's most famous celebrity chefs, who dropped into the restaurant a few times. I had a friend, Paul, who worked for Nick, and he suggested I have a chat with him. That resulted in Nick offering me the position of Executive Head Chef when his restaurant reopened in Bridge of Allan which is not far from Stirling in central Scotland.

Back in 2021 his restaurant closed after a disastrous fire. While waiting for it to reopen and helping with the preparations, I was in charge of the kitchen at the restaurant in Nick's Cooking School. I was quite pleased when he said to me that the quality of the food and the cooking had 'gone up a level' while I'd been working there.

The restaurant in Bridge of Allan, called simply *Nairn's*, reopened in 2023 and I worked with an excellent head chef called Andy Turnbull. When *Nairn's* first opened, it served small plates for sharing. But that didn't work out, the customers didn't like it and we changed to a la carte: starters, main course, and dessert. You must listen to what your customers are telling you and that's why we changed.

After a successful time with *Nairn's*, I returned to *Six by Nico* at the beginning of 20224 in a regional executive chef role, managing all the Scotland sites.

Advice

Show commitment. Get by in your twenties – its ok then. The money will eventually come. The first time I was head chef was far too early; I wasn't ready for it. So, take your time but work hard and gather as much experience as you can. Befriend other chefs, get to know them well and don't be afraid to ask for help.

Have a look at restaurants on Instagram and if a place takes your fancy have your dinner in it. Soak up the atmosphere and taste the food. If both are good, ask if you can have a trial in the kitchen and see if you'd like to work in that place. But I can't emphasise enough, you must show commitment, otherwise you'll be found out very quickly.

Stephen's favourite dish: My mother-in-law Jayne makes an incredible beef bourguignon with dauphinoise potatoes. That's my favourite.

Stephen's favourite wine: A lovely Cote de Rhone that goes well with the beef bourguignon.

21. FERRIER RICHARDSON: THE CELEBRITY CHEF COMES HOME

Often described as a 'celebrity chef,' Ferrier Richardson is one of Scotland's most well-known chefs. After a varied and astonishing international career, his latest venture is in the east end of Glasgow. He takes time out to recall that career and the lessons learned on the way.

Beginnings

I wanted to be a hotel manager and went to Glasgow College of Food Technology in 1974 to study hotel management. Part of the course involved culinary classes and I found I really enjoyed that. On the back of that I decided I wanted to be a chef more than a hotel manager. My course also included visits to kitchens in places like hotels, including the *Central Hotel* in Glasgow, which in the 1970s was in the Michelin Guide.

During that visit, and just before we were moving on to another department of the hotel, the chef took me aside and said: 'If you're looking for a job here son, come and see me.' Next day, I went to see him, and we ended up agreeing that at the end of my course I'd work in the kitchen of the *Central* while going back to the College for a day release each week.

However, six months into that, the *Central* took me aside and said: 'we don't think this is the career for you.' They basically thought I wasn't going to cut it. The problem for me was, in my honest opinion, I thought the lunatics were running the asylum. My parents were very loving and provided me with a stable upbringing, but I could also take discipline as I had been in the Boy's Brigade and was awarded my Queen's Badge. What I couldn't understand, even at the tender age of 16, was the needless and merciless bullying behaviour of some people in that kitchen. That kind of behaviour, stemming from the head chef down, has been rife in some kitchens for decades.

Anyway, after receiving that talk, I walked the short distance to the *Albany Hotel,* which was the first plush, modern large-scale hotel in the city. I was offered a job in the kitchen that day and worked in the *Albany* for the next two-and-a-half years. There I found my spiritual home and some good mentors who put me on the right track, particularly Edouard Hari, the executive head chef who was a young man in his 30s and had just come up from London.

Going international

I really enjoyed working at the *Albany* and it gave me invaluable experience. But six months before I was due to finish my apprenticeship, I knocked on Edward's door and announced that when it was completed in a few months' time, I wanted to work abroad. I think he was stunned at the audacity of a young boy at 18 telling him, effectively, thanks but when I finish my time, I'm out of here!

He didn't take umbrage with me, and using his international contacts, gave me the choice of working in one of three hotels. The first was the *Hiton* in West Berlin, which because it was surrounded by East Germany and the Soviet Bloc, you got paid a bonus for working in. Or there was the *St Moritz Palace* in Switzerland, which I did some research on, and it reminded me too much of the *Central* in Glasgow. Finally, there was the *Intercontinental* in Geneva which was owned by the US airline Pan Am at that time. I choose Geneva.

Very quickly, I became homesick. It was the first time I'd been away from home and my family and on my own in a flat. After a few months I walked into the chef's office, a hard man named Rene Rastello, who had a reputation of being one of the toughest chefs in the business, but also a fair man. I told him that my father was dying, and I had to go back home.

God forgive me, my father wasn't dying but I was desperate to go home. The chef saw right through me, and I opened up and told him the truth: I was a young guy dreadfully homesick. After that, each morning I went into his office, we shook hands and he asked me how I was and that was all I needed, support and encouragement. After that it was fine, and I stayed there for just under a year.

Back home and making a mark

After Geneva, I came back to Glasgow and worked at the *Fountain Restaurant* under a chef named George Quar who was a fantastic man manager and great team leader, but probably not the best chef in the world. Just as I was about to turn 22, the restaurant's owners announced they were transferring Geroge to another of their venues. They offered me the position of chef at the *Fountain,* and it would be down to my performance in the kitchen as to whether George came back as chef. He never did.

Becoming chef was a huge learning curve for me. I was a young bright chef eager to innovate and my priority was to put great food on a plate, but not necessarily concerned with the details of silver service which George would have been. In other words, I was probably, at this stage of my life, better as a cook than as a manager.

The next stage in my career was when the renowned hotelier and restaurant owner, Ken McCulloch, offered to buy the *Fountain*. That came to nothing, but while he was negotiating with the owners, he had a chat with me. Something must have lodged in the back of his mind because when he decided to buy a restaurant called the *Buttery*, he approached me and asked me If I'd work for him. I liked what I saw of him and left to work with him.

But things now moved quite fast. The day the *Buttery* opened in 1982 was the same day McCulloch bought over a well-established Glasgow restaurant called the *Rogano* and he asked me to manage that too. So, at the age of 26, I was running two of Glasgow's most prestigious restaurants. And it didn't stop there. McCulloch also bought over premises in the West End of Glasgow and converted them into a five-star hotel and restaurant called *One Devonshire Gardens*. I was tasked with running all three venues. I did assist with the design of the kitchen at *One Devonshire Gardens*, but I never cooked there because I now decided that it was time to run my own place. I told Ken this and we parted amicably.

A new venture

Working with a business partner, Hugh McShannon, who'd been general manager at the *Rogano*, I focused on starting a new venture, *October* in what can best be described as a leafy, prosperous suburb on the outskirts of Glasgow called Bearsden. Before opening we wanted to build an extension at the back of the premises which had three owners: a bank, an accountant upstairs, and us. The three of us were pouring money into a pot to build this extension, but the problem was that the accountant kept delaying things for months.

Hugh and I had given up two good jobs and we were both driving Porsches, but we were actually going down to the Job Centre and signing on the dole as all our savings were going into the business. Eventually, we had to sell the Porsches to raise more money for the restaurant. I must be the only head chef in Glasgow who's gone from owning a Porsche to buying a Transcard!

People often think when you own a business that you've made it, you're wealthy and don't realise you've put your neck on the line, taken great risks, secured loans on the basis of your assets, including your house, to get that business up and running.

The extension took ages, but we improvised and opened anyway. I painted the walls white and cooked in the kitchen using a six-ring oven, of which only four rings worked and a grill which only half-worked. On Fridays and Saturdays, I was bringing crockery from my own house into the place to supplement the limited supplies in the restaurant. Despite that, *October*, won Scottish Newcomer of the year in 1988. It was quite a difference going from the sophistication and facilities of *One Devonshire Gardens*, the *Buttery*, and the *Rogano* to working in those conditions. But it just goes to show, if you serve good food and provide excellent service, people will come.

We worked on the renovation and made the restaurant light and airy with original artwork on the walls. This was new for Glasgow and made the place even more appealing. Bearsden is a relatively wealthy area, so we had a good, solid customer base on our doorstep, as well as a wide range of people from far and wide. At its height, you had to book five or six weeks in advance to secure a table on Friday and Saturday nights. We were busy every night of the week. We had a great team, and it was the most satisfying time of my career. I had recently married; my two children were born, and everything just seemed to come together.

With the success of *October*, we opened another site, *October Café*, in the upmarket Princess Square mall on Buchanan Street. That did reasonably well, but the site had its challenges, and the Mall was a difficult place to make money.

Going Stateside

Then I got head hunted by Hilton Hotels who were opening their first five-star hotel in Glasgow. Initially they approached me to run the fine dining restaurant at the hotel. My response was why would I want to do that when I've already got two restaurants of my own. Instead, I proposed they let me work in their new Glasgow hotel for two years as executive chef and then I would work as executive chef in their five-star *Park Lane Hotel* in London. That was my real goal; to use Glasgow as a stepping stone to London. They agreed to that.

I hated it, right from the get-go. It was corporate and soulless. I felt everybody was out for themselves and didn't care what the grand design or vision was. I had always worked with people like Ken McCulloch and Hugh McShannon and others who did have that vision. Now, some people do enjoy working as chefs in hotels, but I couldn't take to it. It wasn't for me.

I parted from Hilton and my next venture was a restaurant called *Yes* in the city centre, which was also a success as well as a few other places I opened, including one in Edinburgh. But my biggest venture and investment at that time was *Eurasia*, a large restaurant which I poured three-quarters of a million pounds into.

The context to this is important. I was doing a lot of promotional work in the US, especially New York and I grew to love the city. I was even negotiating with Johnny Walker, the whisky people, to open a place in the Rockefeller Center.

I could see the US as being where I wanted to move. The upshot was with *Eurasia*, I took my eye off the ball and left certain individuals in charge which I shouldn't have, with the result it imploded, and as the named head person, I was left holding the bag. It was hard both financially and mentally and took the wind out of my sails because up to then I'd known nothing but success.

To compound matters the New York venture fell through because there was an old prohibition era law in the States which doesn't allow drinks producers to operate licensed premises. The intention had been for the restaurant to have a whisky bar selling, of course, Johnny Walker. When the lawyers got wind of that they were alarmed and said: 'no, there's a link with the Johnny Walker brand' and put the kybosh on it.

However, I did eventually open a restaurant in the US, in a place called Winter Park just outside Orlando. I had a house there for eight years and my kids used to go to school in Scotland and fly across to Florida which they enjoyed. I kept the house on for longer but closed the restaurant after three years.

There followed a period when I was doing a variety of jobs. I helped James Mortimer, the Glasgow nightclub owner who'd just bought over the *Rogano*, to refurbish it. I opened a place in southern Spain in a town which I loved, and I also did consultancy for a group of people in Egypt and opened three restaurants for them in Cairo.

The President's Chef

Then I received a cryptic phone call from an agency in London saying they had a job which they couldn't tell me anything about, but they thought it would be worth my while to come down to London and speak with the people involved. I was intrigued and flew down and they paid for my flight.

My directions were to go a large house off Berkeley Square in London which was being renovated. There I was interviewed by a chap called Bruce Newson, who had been number 2 chef to Queen Elizabeth. Thirty minutes into the interview he revealed who the job was for. It was the personal chef for the President and First Lady of Gabon in west Africa. The only reason I'd ever heard of Gabon was that the Glasgow Rangers player, Danial Cousin, had come from Gabon. I was offered the position based on trying it for three months to see if it worked out for both parties. I accepted and stayed for four-and-a-half years.

Apart from working for myself it was the best job I ever had outside Glasgow. As well as the President's personal chef, I was responsible for running some of his houses scattered across the world in places like Marrakesh and Paris. In each house I oversaw a team. I was part of the President's inner circle and flew everywhere on private jets. I also became a member of the *Chef des Chefs des Chefs* an exclusive club open only to the personal chefs of heads of state.

I met President Obama, and I was in Buckingham Palace the night before the Queen travelled up to Glasgow to open the Commonwealth Games in 2014. I spoke to both her and Prince Phillip for ten minutes and her personal chef, Mark, told me she rarely spoke to anyone for that length of time. She appeared intrigued at how a boy from Glasgow could end up being a personal chef for a head of state in Africa. I'll treasure that memory of my ten minutes with the Queen. All told, that was a fantastic time.

Tragedy & Recovery

Then it all came crashing down. I was lying on a beach outside the capital of Gabon when I received a call from Glasgow informing me that my younger brother, Simon, had been murdered. The President's people arranged a flight for me, and I was back home in next to no time. In Glasgow, the brutal reality struck home. My mother had dementia and Simon was her principal carer.

I stayed for his funeral and went back to Gabon. Four weeks later my wife phoned to tell me that, even though my mother had dementia, she was aware of Simon's death and was reacting very badly to it and I needed to get back, which I did. My wife and I looked after her for a short period, but she died on Christmas Day. Within the space of six weeks, I'd lost my brother and mother.

Back in Gabon, after my mother's funeral, I worked for four weeks, but realised those two calamitous events had really taken its toll. I saw the President and First Lady on a daily basis, and I was able to have a frank conversation with them where I said I couldn't go on any longer. They were completely understanding, and I left their service to return home.

For the next two years I did nothing, apart from a little consultancy work, including property development. I didn't lift a knife. After the two years, I went back to Spain where I tried to do some property development and consultancy but spent most of the time on the beach reading loads of books, relaxing and slowly getting my head back together.

After that, I spent two lucrative years, one in Marbella in Spain, working with two restaurant owners and their teams into transforming their restaurants into two very profitable businesses, which I earned a good amount from, until I was headhunted again by a London agency. This time I was recruited to be the personal chef of the world's leading expert on osteoporosis, Professor John Kanis. He was based in Surrey but would travel frequently to lectures across the world. When he was away, I would go back to Spain. I ended up spending an average of a month working with the professor and when he was off on his travels, about six weeks back in Spain.

It was a good arrangement for both of us until covid came along in 2020 and changed the world. At the same time, my daughter was pregnant, and my wife felt strongly that she wanted to come back to Glasgow for the birth of our grandson and that's what we did.

However, I can't sit on my backside for long and I started looking for a place to open in the city centre on a similar basis to the *October Café*, *Yes* or *Eurasia*. But people I respected in hospitality advised me against the city centre; business wasn't great there, but the outer areas of the city were performing better.

Moving east

As it happens, when I'm in Glasgow, I've spent most of my married life living in an area called Mount Vernon on the city's eastern outskirts. I knew the area well and know most of the characters who lived there. The large hospitality company Greene King had some premises they owned for sale in the district, and I put a bid in.

Some of the bids, including mine, were well over the asking price. Apparently, Greene King were taken aback by the quality of the bids and realised they were about to sell a place which could have a lot of potential. The upshot was, they didn't accept any of the bids and instead, advertised for a tenant.

There were 55 applicants, which were whittled down to about five, including me, who were interviewed. I was the successful applicant. I was very fortunate because as the selection process was going on there was a lot of adverse publicity about how badly pub companies were treating their tenants. The deal I got was very favourable: a ten-year lease without being tied to buying only Greene King products. I do buy some of their brands, but I'm not confined to them so, I'm free to shop around for good deals.

We spent a year designing and renovating the premises, which we called the *East End Fox*, and is located on a busy road junction. Finally, we opened in October 2022 (I do seem to have an affinity to October) and the site has done well, winning a number of awards including Scottish Pub of the Year and runner up for British Pub of the Year.

Recently, we were celebrating my son's 40th birthday and we went to New York to celebrate. While there we were also checking some bars and restaurants to see what we could adopt for the *East End Fox*. We also paid a visit to Washington DC and the White House courtesy of one of my friends who is executive chef there. It was while we were in the Rose Garden, just outside President Biden's office that I received a phone call. It was from the Sultan of Brunei's office asking if I would look after the Sultan's family in August 2023 when they were staying in the south of Spain. I agreed and had a pleasant time with the family.

Now the point of relating this is that on social media I'm posting pictures of my son, Keith and myself in the White House followed by looking after the Sultan of Brunei. It lends a bit of prestige both for the restaurant and our customers. I can picture one of our regular characters in the *East End Fox* thinking: 'Here's a guy who cooks for the Sultan of Brunei and cooks for me an ordinary person from the east end of Glasgow!' Win win.

Advice

You need to have a passion for this business. You just can't be in it for the money. If you think of all the successful restaurant operators in Glasgow that are not part of the big chains, yes, they're motivated by money, but it's not the whole story. You would need to be insane to put in the hours, the time spent away from your family, meeting all the obstacles this business will throw at you if you were not passionate about it.

Ferrier's favourite dish: Mince and potatoes. I've travelled all over the world and when I've phoned my wife from Istanbul, China, wherever, and she asks me, 'what do you want to eat, when you come home?' my reply was always a nice plate of mince and tatties. That's the kind of food we serve at the *East End Fox* which I describe as elevated comfort food. I include in that bracket steak pie, fish and chips, sausage n' mash and so on. It's good solid fare which is becoming more popular now and I firmly believe we're doing it to a far higher standard than a lot of the pub chains.

Ferrier's favourite wine: I like Malbec. I think South America has some great wines.

22. BRIAN SCANLAN: CAMERON HOUSE, ON THE BONNIE BANKS

Another prominent Scottish chef who's worked his way up from kitchen porter, Brian Scanlan is the Executive Head Chef at the exclusive Cameron House Hotel on Loch Lomond. His road to the bonnie banks is outlined here.

Beginnings

I grew up the east end of Glasgow in the 1980s. There wasn't a lot of home cooking and sit-down dinners in my family, when I was a kid. My mother worked three jobs and cooking was probably the last thing on her mind. I wasn't in the house much anyway always playing football till I was called in late in the evening, so any dinner that was left wasn't the best! So, I learned how to cook for myself very quickly. I grew up in a household of four brothers; the fact that three of them became chefs probably tells its own story.

I would later hear all these stories about chefs having memories of drooling over their granny's apple pie which inspired them to become a chef. That never happened in my house.

My career started at 17 with a summer job in 1994 as a kitchen porter (KP) at the *Millennium hotel,* an old British Transport hotel run by a strict, experienced head chef called James Anderston. That was a very disciplined and traditional cooking kitchen who rarely took on KPs as chefs, but I kept on asking Mr Anderston if I could get a chef's position and eventually, he relented, and I worked there for four-and-a-half years.

I took to it quite quickly, I enjoyed cooking, the buzz and the camaraderie with the boys. It was like an apprenticeship in cooking, learning from each section until you finally got to the sauce section. I think I learned more about the importance of organisation and working fast with efficiency and hygienically. From there I moved on to the *Moat House* for two years under the Executive chef, James Murphy.

I learnt a lot there about hotels and how they operated. I ran the *Mariner* restaurant which was two rosette standards at the time. After a few years, I decided I wanted to see the world and got a job on a cruise liner, the QE2 no less which had been built on the Clyde many years before.

Cooking on the high seas

A chance to see the world I thought. Yes, you did see the world, but it was very hard work, but something I personally enjoyed. Fourteen-hour shifts, seven days per week with four months on, one month off. Not many people could handle the work at sea, people would drop off very quickly, most citing seasickness. But it was mostly down to how hard an environment it was to work in.

Preparing and cooking 200 covers for breakfasts, lunches and dinners and nonstop partying every night weren't for the weak. Every day was a battle I referred to my time on the QE2 in a quote: "kill or be killed". Everything you needed to do the job was difficult to secure, ingredients, equipment etc; it became like a military operation to attain. But we achieved them by any means necessary; midnight raids into other kitchens were not unheard off.

There were seven restaurants on the ship, of which the top one was the *Queen's Grill* and 150 chefs to service those restaurants. I worked in the kitchen of a British themed style restaurant where the menu changed daily and only served lunch. There were five of us in that kitchen: an Englishman, Irishman, Welshman, a guy from Thailand and a Scotsman, me. I don't think the Thai fellow knew a word the rest of us were saying, though he laughed a lot, whether it with us or at us I don't know.

The five of us would get the stores at five pm and prepare for a thousand covers buffet style lunches for the next day. We'd get fresh stores at each port which would supply us to the next port. We got pretty good and fast at this and were normally the first chefs in the crew bar. The Filipinos' storeman supplied the food to the kitchens and if we paid them, they'd get the supplies to us faster, so we were able to prepare the food quicker and then have time to go offshore when we were at a port.

On my last two cruise assignments I was placed in the *Queen's Grill* which I was recommended for. The highest paying passengers dined there, and no expense was spared. Only the most expensive items of food were served with three chefs on a section for service each day. If a particularly rare item was not on the menu, guests would sometimes order for it to be delivered to the ship by helicopter; we didn't have to worry about a budget.

It was a great experience working there because the food standards were of such a high quality. The downside was it was a more difficult kitchen to work in, and time off wasn't the best compared to the other restaurants. However, it gave me a great learning experience in different cuisines cooked very well.

Overall, I found the cruise liners a worthwhile career experience and I would advise any chef to try it for at least a year. It will build up your endurance and the ability to work at speed in a very busy environment. I saw people breakdown after two weeks, desperate to get off the ship. When I hear chefs complaining about working ten days straight, I think back to then, but we never had problems getting staff.

The money was good and was virtually tax free. I did that for a year over three cruises and decided that was enough for me.

I came back to Glasgow and worked under James Murphy again, this time at the new *Hilton* hotel on William Street where there was a good strong team. It had its own butcher and there were really high standards all round, no scrimping or cost cutting. That was easily the best hotel I'd worked in Glasgow at that time.

After two years with the *Hilton,* and just under ten years working non-stop in high-pressured environments I was unsure if I wanted to continue as a chef for the rest of my career. I looked at the older seniors above me in kitchens and how they managed people and their lives, and I thought I don't want to end up like that. Looking back, I was probably suffering from burn out and needed a change to refresh, which I would advise to any chef.

Taking up coaching

I've always had a keen interest in sport and fitness and being a decent football player, I decided to go to college and study HND sports coaching. From there I went on to Strathclyde University and studied sports science. I never left cooking though as I worked part-time in many kitchens to support my studies. In my heart of hearts, I knew I'd be back full-time in the kitchens at some point.

One of the benefits I gained from those years in coaching was learning how to manage and get the best out of people by adapting to different personalities. I sincerely believe it's allowed me to develop good teams by getting the best out of each person. In my early days' kitchens were an all-male environment, not many women worked in kitchens, and it was often a brutal place to work. Now it's a different mentality and kitchens have changed. A lot more women work in kitchens and that has improved the atmosphere and the working conditions for chefs.

My time coaching made me realise that working with kitchen teams is very similar to coaching sports teams. It's about having a strategy, a game plan, sticking to it and building a team which works well together to carry that plan out. That's the approach I now take to developing people in kitchens and it's worked well for me. Its best summed up as: you're only as good as your team in the kitchen.

I went to university at the age of 26 after nine years in the trade. I probably would have made head chef quicker if I hadn't gone to higher education, but I was glad I took the break as it did benefit me in the end.

Back to the trade

After university I worked in a call centre promoting healthy eating for a while when I got a call from an executive chef I knew, called Stewart Goldie. He told me there was a head chef position going in a new hotel in Largs, a popular seaside town on the Clyde coast which gets incredibly busy in sunny weather as it's only an hour from Glasgow. Well, I thought, the only way is up, give it a try.

The owner had spent a lot of money renovating the hotel and wanted to change the perception of Largs. It was busy from the opening of the hotel, and they were queues at the door in the summer. Within the kitchen and restaurant there was a close-knit circle of people from the local area. This creates problems right away; an outsider coming in and trying to change things doesn't usually go down well. I had to employ a lot of the coaching and psychology techniques to get them to do what I asked. I got there eventually but it was a challenge. The greatest compliment was, when I went back down there five years later, and they were still doing things the way I had showed them.

From there I became head chef at *Epicure's* in the Hyndland area of the West End of Glasgow which was owned then by a chap called Lawrence McManus. It was probably the busiest restaurant in that area and, again, there were queues at the door. Previously, Hyndland had been very residential with no hospitality venues, but after *Epicures* opened and was a success, other restaurants and cafes popped up close by.

Before *Epicures* it had been hotel kitchens, I'd mainly worked in. This was the first proper restaurant I'd been in. After I'd taken the time out to study, I decided I'd wanted to try different types of kitchens to build up as much experience as possible. *Epicures* was an all-day brasserie type restaurant open from eight am till late with different menus through the day from breakfast to dinner and it was constantly busy.

Those were challenging conditions to develop a team and a lot of the kitchen staff and chefs couldn't cope with the pressure. It took about eighteen months to develop a good team.

From there I moved on to the *Finneston* in that area of Glasgow to the west of the city centre that has exploded with cafes, bars and restaurant since the turn of the century and the opening of the nearby Exhibition Centre complex, including since 2013 the Hydro which can accommodate huge acts. I started in the *Finneston* as the Hydro was just opening so it was another constantly busy venue. I'd never worked in a fish restaurant before and it was good experience to work with the suppliers daily, order in fresh produce and get to know it very well. I could also develop the chefs there who were new, and I had a free rein with the menu.

My next move was further into the West End to a place called the *Bothy* where I stayed for a couple of years. By this time, I decided I wanted to work in large-scale, high-volume brasserie type places so I had the opportunity to move to London and work with Corbyn King, one of the most famous restaurant groups in Britain and one of the best I've ever worked with. They treated everyone with respect and courtesy from KPs up to head chefs.

Between three cities

On my first day at Corbin King, one of the founders Jeremy King, who oversees seven iconic restaurants in London, greeted me personally and that was indicative of the way they operated the business as highly professional restauranters. It was small things like never forgetting your birthday and always making time to talk to you which made all the difference.

There's a lot of charlatans in this business who take advantage of people, especially young people, so it's important to work with companies and senior managers that treat people with respect.

One thing that stood out for me about this company was the focus they had on personal development and training of their staff. This was shown in the high standard and attention to detail they had towards service in all the restaurants They performed a 360-degree review on you which pinpointed your weaknesses and how to overcome them but also highlighted your strengths. By contrast, most companies in this business hire chefs and leave them in busy kitchens without any support or development plan whatsoever.

I stayed there for a few years opening a restaurant in Islington in London called *Bellanger*, which achieved a Michelin Bib Gourmand award in its first year. While I was at the *Bellanger,* I was headhunted by Mark Askew, executive chef of the Ivy Group to be head chef of a new site that's was opening in Buchanan Street in Glasgow city centre. It was a great opportunity; I'd been three years in London and fancied coming back home.

However, the Ivy Group had an issue with planning permission for the site, and they decided to delay reapplying for at least a year. I was left with no job in London or Glasgow and six weeks to find the next rent for my flat.

I applied for a job with a company called *Hawksmoor*, a large, popular steak restaurant in London, who were opening a site in Edinburgh.

My application was successful. All their meat was well-sourced and butchered inside the premises and made into large steaks cooked on massive charcoal grills in the middle of the restaurant. This was another new part of the business I gained experience in as I'd gone from fish to large-scale brasseries and now it was meat. Again, it was tough cooking steaks in the middle of a busy restaurant with all eyes on you while throwing six rib-eye steaks onto a charcoal grill and keeping a careful watch on it. Not the easiest of tasks.

We tried to recruit staff locally, but it was just before the Edinburgh Festival, and we couldn't find enough experienced staff. When we opened, we had 15 staff compared to the 26 we needed, of whom only six had any previous experience in catering.

Despite that we went straight into doing 250 covers a night and I was personally working about 110 hours per week. My physical training on the QE2 served me well because I was commuting from Glasgow, catching the last train home from Edinburgh, snatching a few hours, then travelling back on an early morning train. You need to be really fit to do this job otherwise it will burn you out physically and emotionally.

While at the *Hawksmoor* in Edinburgh, the Ivy Group got back in touch to inform me that they were now ready to open their site in Glasgow and would I still be interested in being head chef. Well as a Glasgow boy the chance to open a place in my hometown with such a prestigious name was irresistible. Besides, it meant I could cut out all that travelling.

The *Ivy* in Glasgow opened in 2019 and quickly had the highest turnover of any restaurant in the group outside London and Manchester It was crazily busy from the get-go. On any given Saturday, you could do between 700-900 covers. It was a relatively big kitchen with 35 chefs working in it which is a lot more than most comparable restaurants would have, but you needed it because it was full on.

When you're managing a team the size of that, the quality of the food is important but so is your man management skills. You need to know who to push, who not to, who are the superstars and so on. That's when all those coaching skills I'd picked up became so useful. There are some amazing, probably better skilled chefs than me at cooking, but they couldn't manage a kitchen of 40 staff. They could manage a kitchen with a staff of six in a specialised fine dining venue with a limited menu and restricted opening hours. That's why I always say there's room for everybody in hospitality; you just have adjust to what a particular restaurant is trying to do. Restaurants fail when they're unclear about what they're doing or who their market is.

On the bonnie banks

I stayed with the *Ivy* through most of lockdown which put a halt to the group's intention to open a second venue in Glasgow where I would have hoped to have been promoted up to area chef. Instead, I moved to join the team at the prestigious *Cameron House* on the bonny banks of Loch Lomond in December 2022 as executive sous chef before becoming executive head chef.

There are six dining areas in the hotel. One is the *Great Sports Bar* which serves upmarket bar food. Then there's the *Cameron Grill,* which is our restaurant serving breakfast, and dinner 2 rosette standard. There's a new bar called the *Tavern sports Bar* which serves upmarket fast food, that's very popular and can easily serve 300 covers on a Saturday. We serve afternoon tea in the lobby bar and have a meeting and event space for over 600 covers. The *Boathouse* which is a seafood restaurant can also do 250 covers per service. Last of all is the *Cameron Golf Club and Spa*, another busy venue in the resort serving breakfast, lunch and dinner.

I'm in charge of all the kitchens at the hotel and resort and manage a total of 55 chefs. Each venue has a head chef which the senior team and I manage.

When I started, there was 35 chefs and I've recruited a lot more since and I now oversee the 55 chefs. They are a great team and have worked well with each other since I have taken over. We're well placed now to take *Cameron House* back to the top and I look forward to playing a major part in that.

Advice

My daughter Niamh told me recently she would like to be a chef. She's a good cook and would have no problems getting a job. I told her it's a very rewarding career with so many opportunities attached to it.

However, it's a very consuming job if you let it take over you. It's not just about what happens in the kitchen. You're often thinking about it after you go home; and as soon as you wake up, sometimes it can be hard to switch off. This is more than just a job and it demands a high degree of commitment. My enjoyment of fitness allows me to let the stress of the day leave me, and I'm thankful for that.

I said to my daughter, the best thing to do if you want to become a chef, is start at the bottom and learn everything you can but stay at a low level for as long as possible and enjoy the journey not the process. The higher up you go the pressure gets intense and you need to be really experienced and know what you're doing to handle that.

My most enjoyable time was as a commis chef or *chef de partie* because the pressure was not as great, and you just did what you were asked to do. Take your time, then try and aim higher.

Brian's favourite dish: Lasagne because it was the only thing my mother could make that would get me in from playing football at night. An authentic "east end lasagne" I would call it.

Brian's favourite wine: I'm not really a wine drinker, but I do like Amarone.

23. AURELIEN MOUREZ: OX & FINCH, TAPAS WITH A DIFFERENCE

From the Alps to the West End, of Glasgow, Aurelian Mourez and his team at the Ox & Finch are serving traditional dishes in new and innovative ways. Given how constantly busy this restaurant is, Glasgow appears to approve. Read more here.

Beginnings

I come from a little county in France known as Jura which is famous for its wines and cheeses. My grandfather was a wine grower and part of a co-operative producing and selling wines and cheeses. I was brought up in an environment where there was always good and fresh food around me. Stimulated by this, from an early age I wanted to do something creative with food and becoming a chef seemed to be the best way to achieve that goal.

When I was 15, I started hospitality school where I specialised in butchery and pastry catering for four years. After leaving there I worked in various kitchens around France including Burgundy and the Alps before I moved to work in the Caribbean Island of St Martin which is half-Dutch and half-French. I worked there for a year and when I came back to France, I appreciated the importance of learning English as this was the international language of hospitality and catering.

Coming to Glasgow

I decided I wanted to work outside France and immerse myself in the local language and started applying for catering jobs abroad. One of the first to reply was from Glasgow; a position for a pastry chef in the kitchen at a hotel called *Abode* in Glasgow under Micheal Caines. My application was successful, and I arrived in Glasgow in 2010.

I had very little command of English when I first came here, and I had to pick it up quickly in the first few months. While working in *Abode* I met my wife, who was then working in front of house at the hotel. She was the reason I stayed in Glasgow, and she now works in tourism.

After *Abode* I worked with the Glasgow restaurateur Brian Maule for a year and then I went to *Cael Bruch*, a fine dining Michlin Star restaurant in the West End of the city where I also stayed for a year.

Ox and Finch

My wife and I went back to France for a short period. While there I was offered a position with the *Ox and Finch*, a fine dining restaurant which was also located in the West End of Glasgow. I came back to the city with my wife and started at the *Ox and Finch* as *chef de partie* and worked my way up.

There's no specific style of cooking at the restaurant. We take classic dishes and combine them in new and innovative ways, incorporating and mixing different elements. We have a very collaborative approach to creating the dishes and we all work closely together. There are 14 chefs in the kitchen. We're open seven days and usually there will be three chefs on at any one time. We have 250 covers over the course of a day (about 70 at any one time and we're open from 12 to 10pm every day). There's also a private dining section downstairs. It's a high-volume, very busy restaurant but we do everything to maintain good quality and high standards.

I've been working here for nine years and in the 13 years I've been working in the city I've noticed a greater appetite on the part of both customers and chefs for greater diversity and trying different ingredients. Before there was a tendency for restaurants to serve similar style dishes, but now there's much more variety. I would even go so far to say there's been a revolution in food tastes and a desire to experiment with different food styles across the city.

I've also noticed how kitchens have become more relaxed places over the last few years. They could be quite confrontational. Now they're more collaborative, less harsh. I think a lot of the younger chefs have brought this new approach with them and I believe it works better for developing teamwork and supporting people to get the best out of them.

Advice

If you want to be a chef, be patient. There's so much to learn different styles, different techniques, so much variety of foods and ways of cooking them. Take as much as you can from everyone around you.

Aurelien's favourite dish: Veal sweetbreads with Morel mushroom sauce.

Aurelien's favourite wine: Vin Jaune, a beautiful white from my home area of Jura, delicious with the veal sweetbreads and mushroom sauce.

24. ASIF ALI: SHISH MAHAL, A GLASGOW INDIAN LEGEND

The Shish Mahal is a Glasgow landmark and Asif Ali tells the story of how over three generations his family built this curry colossus.

Beginnings

My dad and grandfather came over from Pakistan after the Second World War. My grandfather worked in the jute mills in Dundee, making sacks for a few years, before around 1950, moving to Glasgow and working in the shipyards on the Clyde.

After a few years he'd saved enough money to bring my grandmother over to Scotland. That was most unusual in those days. The convention was for the man to send back money to provide for the family and bring the sons over while the women would stay at home.

My grandmother was NOT like a lot of Pakistani women. She was a strong formidable woman, the power in the house, essentially a matriarch. She would order my father and uncle to wrestle each other to see who was the strongest!

After my grandmother came over, my grandfather opened the *Greengates Asian Restaurant* on Bank Street in Glasgow's West End which operated for three years. He had some business partners who just regarded the restaurant as a cash machine. They would come in, fill their wallets with the takings and walk away; they had no other interest in the business. My grandfather thought this was not good enough, closed the restaurant and reopened around the corner on Gibson Street under a new name, *Shish Mahal*.

This time he ran the place with no partners or outside interference. He didn't employ a chef. Instead, my no-nonsense grandmother became a chef and my father, after working at the Sher Brothers' wholesale business during the day, would work in the restaurant in the evenings.

After finishing he would walk from the West End back to the Gorbals across the Clyde where he stayed with his uncle and cousins. He would get up early the next morning and open the cash and carry. The Sher Brothers and their cash-and-carry business went on to become a famous household name in Glasgow.

Just before Pakistan became independent from Britain, the Sher Brother's grandfather lived in a village where an army brigadier had redistributed land among the local people. The only problem was their grandfather didn't receive any land. He complained relentlessly to the brigadier, who exasperated by him asked a local landowner to give him some. However, the land he did receive was the village rubbish heap. Realising the land was worthless he gave the land back to the owner in exchange for enough money to send his two sons to the UK, to Glasgow. That was the origin of the Sher Brothers' cash and carry empire, who went on to become one of the richest Asian Families in Scotland.

For six years my grandfather ran the *Shish Mahal* as a family business, and it steadily grew in popularity. My grandmother was not a trained chef, and she used the traditional recipes and ingredients she would cook with back home. Gibson Street was right next to Glasgow University and a lot of Asian students came in and really appreciated the authentic food. They told their Scottish friends, and the restaurant rapidly gained a good customer base.

The *Shish Mahal* and the Invention of Chicken Tikka Masala

After six years my grandfather asked my father to work full-time in the restaurant. At this time, he also employed the first non-family member, Molly, as a waitress.

Up to this point, the business had been ticking over, but once dad started working full-time there and Molly was on board, it really took off. And then came my dad's invention…chicken tikka masala.

One night a regular customer, a bus driver, came in. He was in a bad mood and ordered chicken curry. When his order came, he returned it complaining it was 'too dry.' My father had a stomach ulcer so, ironically could not eat spicey food. Dad was a first-generation immigrant, and everything was about saving money, so he used to buy tins of condensed tomato soup which he would eke out for his lunch and dinner.

When Molly brought the chicken curry back with the complaint it was too dry, my father instructed the chef to pour half a can of the condensed tomato soup my father used into the curry. Molly took it back out to him and came back reporting that the customer was now raving about how 'fantastic' it was! The following day that customer came back again asking for that 'incredible dish you served me.' Back in the kitchen, my dad and the chef scratched their heads trying to think what that was before remembering it was the chicken curry with the tomato soup poured all over it. They gave him it again and he was just as happy with it. He came back the next day demanding the same dish and the next…

After a few weeks of this, my dad and the chef looked at what the ingredients were in that condensed soup, and they worked out it was the cream and tomatoes which were bringing the distinctive flavour to the chicken. As ever, conscious about saving money, they cut out the tins of soup and made the tomato and cream sauce themselves and added it to the chicken curries. It went down a storm.

There was no "science" about it or market research or anything like that. All these families, whether they be Indian, Chinese, Italian or whatever, all came from poor backgrounds and had to innovate with little money. They would have to make do with what they had and assess carefully what their customers liked and what worked. It was out of that, that some great dishes were born which became part of the diet of the British people. In our case that was masala.

Expansion and becoming a Glasgow institution.

By the mid-1960s, our original premises on Gibson Street were now too small for us and we swapped with Fionda Olive oil company who were in much bigger premises in the same street. The new site was over shop units, much bigger than the previous place, effectively an entire block. The *Shish Mahal* or the '*Shish*' as it was known became a landmark on the street.

My family bought a townhouse at the corner of Gibson Street and Bank Street, a few hundred feet from the *Shish*. I was born in 1972 and my earliest memories were of the restaurant; I could see it from my bedroom. My father didn't want me to go into the restaurant. He wanted me to be a lawyer, or doctor, the usual professions fathers want their sons to enter. But I wasn't interested. I *did* go on to university to study hotel management, but the restaurant was my life.

To me entering the restaurant was like going into Disneyland, or even better, the scene in Goodfellas where Ray Liotta takes his girlfriend into the restaurant and the camera follows them as she's introduced to all these people with names like "Johnny NoNo" and "Frankie Two Times". That was how it felt to me. Often restaurant staff are reserved or diffident around the boss's son, but they were so welcoming to me at the *Shish* and always introduced me to the customers, so I got to know them.

Blogging and Consultancy

I started working on odd jobs and part-time in the restaurant at about 11, and became full-time there in 1993, over 30 years. A lot of people in this business will tell you they love restaurants. But I really do. As well as this place, I write a blog called *Alfie FoodWalla* which involves me travelling around the world reviewing restaurants. I run ResExp, a restaurant consultancy for people needing help and assistance with running and scaling their restaurants. I don't just like restaurants, I *LOVE them*. I'm immersed in them. It's my life 24/7.

In relation to my consultancy, I've often found that people look for advice and assistance when it's far too late and the damage is irreversible. You should really look to be seeking help when the business is doing well, but there are signs of trouble emerging on the horizon, not way down the line when there's little that can be done to turn things around.

Even when I'm not working in the restaurant, writing the blog or doing consultancy, I'll spend whatever free time I have on the internet looking at restaurant websites. I never find anything to do with restaurants dull or tedious. And I'm always looking out for new techniques or things I could adapt for the *Shish* because this is a fast-moving trade.

Customers are far more sophisticated now than before. They're on the internet, they watch all those TV programmes on food, interviews with head chefs and so. They've travelled a lot, and they know the ingredients and often the recipes as well. There was a time when you could serve them anything, but that's long gone. Now they want the best and they'll not be quiet about it if they don't get it. Our customers today have much more sophisticated palates.

Advice

First thing is you need to strongly dispel the notion a lot of people have when coming into this business that it's all about fun and an extension of their living room where they can socialise and bring friends. It's NOT. It's a business first and foremost. Once you get rid of that idea the next thing is to ask yourself why you want to start a restaurant. If it's just for the money forget it. Money only comes when there's a load of other things working well together.

You need to ask yourself basic questions: who is going to be the chef? What experience do they have? What are you going to provide and more importantly what difference are you going to make to what's already out there? The best way of thinking about it is this. Imagine you're driving a car on the motorway while at the same time you're changing the tyres, washing it, fixing the engine, and filling it up with petrol. That's what running a restaurant is like. You will never have the opportunity to park the car and service it; you will always have to drive and service it at the same time. You'll need a strong work ethic and commitment.

However, the reward and sense of satisfaction from running a popular and successful restaurant is like nothing else in the world, despite all the hassles and challenges.

Favourite dish: Believe it or not fish and chips. I steal away occasionally to the *Merchant Fish and Chip shop* on Ingram

Street in the Merchant City to have a delicious fish supper. It's my guilty pleasure.

Favourite drink: We are strictly non-alcoholic, and our favourite drink is water and Diet Coke. Even back in Pakistan, things have evolved, and Diet Coke is the most popular drink.

25. STEFANO GIOVANAZZI: CAFÉ PARMA, KEEPING A FAMILY TRADITION

Stefano's family have served great food in Glasgow for generations at some well-known and well-loved venues. The latest incarnation is Café Parma in the West End. Read this remarkable family history as told by Stefano himself.

Beginnings
In Italy before World War 1, my grandfather's older brother, Eugenio, a quietly ambitious and yet practical man, decided to leave the town of Borgo Val di Taro in the shadow of the Apennine Hills near Parma, Italy filled with uncertainty about the impending war. He told my grandfather,

Giovanni, he was going to Scotland to find a job. When he found one, he said he would write to my grandfather and tell him to come over to join him. His brother ended up in Motherwell working for an Italian immigrant and, true to his word and unfaltering sense of family, he wrote to my grandfather asking him to come over.

My grandfather duly set off by train from his hometown in Italy and made the long pilgrimage through the rich landscape of sun-bleached olive groves and plentiful orchards to the rather bleak, industrial town of Motherwell which would have been a stark contrast to the world he was used to, but like the rest of my family his resilience, adaptability, determination and work ethic would see him through.

My grandfather's brother left for America, not yet recognising the potential here and gave Giovanni his job promising he would see him alright when he had made it in America; the American dream was still vivid then and the lure was just too great to resist. He moved to Philadelphia where sadly, he died but his legacy lives on. In honour of his brother my grandfather named his first chip shop after that city in an area called St George's Cross. Later that chip shop moved to Glasgow's Great Western Road in the city's West End, at Kelvinbridge, and the *Philadelphia* fish and chip shop is still there, doing great business to this day.

In the summer of 1939, under the shadow of the fast-approaching war, my grandfather, Giovanni took my dad, Angelo and my grandmother, Celestina to a family holiday in Italy. He confidently declared that 'this war won't last long, a couple of months at the most. You stay here with our son, and when it's over, I'll come back, and we can return to Scotland.'

It was 1948 before my father was able to get back to Scotland and see his father again.

The first *Philadelphia* was demolished by the Council to make way for the M8 motorway which now snakes through the city. My grandfather passed away and he's buried here in

Glasgow. My father regularly went back to Italy where he met my mum, Maria, and they got married there in 1956 in Borgo Val di Taro.

I have two siblings, Sandro my brother, and my sister, Loredana. I'm the youngest of the three and we were all born in Glasgow.

Creating great Glasgow restaurants

My dad returned, determined and resolute to continue the legacy of his father and uncle and to make a life for himself and my mum Maria. He opened a fish and chip shop in the Woodlands area. He also opened the current *Philadelphia* and sold off the other chip shop and the restaurant in the 1970s. Being the astute and ambitious man that he was, he also bought a car parts business located in premises next door to the *Philadelphia* and converted that into an Italian restaurant called *La Parmigiana*.

That restaurant went on to become a Glasgow institution, but at the time it was fraught with challenge and fate. My mother, Maria, was very unwell with a serious illness in her early forties. Thankfully she survived, but despite her bad health, she insisted my dad go ahead with *La Parmigiana* and a lot of the dishes served in the restaurant were inspired by my mother's traditional cooking back home in the Parma region. They were simple and unpretentious dishes but also hearty, healthy, and full of flavour. It's ironic that original Italian dishes, such as those served up at *La Parmigiana* are now being favoured by trendy restaurants, but overall, there is a fashion for Italian cooking to go back to its roots.

My mother fully recovered and was consistently a supportive, creative, and passionate force behind the success of *La Parmigiana* and beyond.

After many years my dad was awarded a medal from the trade association in Parma in honour of his services to the area in popularising its traditional food products, recipes, and cooking for the people of Scotland.

My dad was a personality; you definitely knew when he was around. One of the regular customers at *La Parmigiana* was Sir Hugh Fraser, a prominent Scottish businessman. Sir Hugh insisted that my dad personally cook him a fish supper. So, my dad donned a white coat, went through to the *Philadelphia* next door, cooked fish and chips and served it to Sir Hugh in the restaurant with a bottle of Chablis on a regular basis.

I was born in Glasgow, went to The High School of Glasgow and studied Italian and French language and literature at Glasgow University. After university I had this romantic notion of going to Italy, of seeing the "old country" so that always sat at the edges of my awareness and sense of self. But first, I had to sample the pleasures of the 1980s and 90s. I moved to London where music and fashion were becoming exciting again, although I still loved all things Italian, especially the food and culture.

When I graduated, I was 21. I moved to London and spent a few years there. I went traveling to Asia and Australia. But eventually, I was drawn back to Glasgow. I didn't want to admit that to myself at first but over time I realised that Glasgow was where I was meant to be – not least I felt the pull of my family and my roots and the delicious food they served.

Back in Glasgow and (almost) getting no satisfaction.

While I was in London, there was a near disastrous incident at *La Parmigiana*. One quiet evening, a People Carrier drew up at the restaurant and a man came out of it, walked into the restaurant, and inquired if there was a table available for six or eight people. The head waiter took it upon himself to regard the customer as far too scruffy and turned him away. Fortunately, my brother Sandro, who was working in the kitchen, ran out and said to the waiter: 'What you doing? You can't turn him away!'

My brother rescued the situation by dashing outside and apologising to the man, saying there had been a mistake and his party was more than welcome to dine there. Within two minutes Mick Jagger, Bill Wyman and the rest of the Rolling Stones and their entourage were sitting at a table being served. Thank goodness my brother was working that night.

I did come back to Glasgow in 1991 and opened *Paperino's* in Sauchiehall Street in November of that year. That was the first venture my brother and I opened on our own. Then we opened *Topolino's* downstairs. The name *Paperino's* was inspired by my travelling experiences. I wanted a name that was easy on the tongue but also sounded Italian. There was a restaurant in Sydney called *Paperino* which was very popular and easy to pronounce and that's where I got the inspiration for the name.

My next venture after that was the *Big Blue* in 1994 which was a downstairs bar/diner on the banks of the river Kelvin right next to both the *Philadelphia* and *La Parmigiana*

At this point I opened *Paperino's West End*, on Byres Road, the most popular street in the West End. That was a big beast all right. I like to be hands on, but this was a large, very busy unit. There were 180 covers and there was a mezzanine floor. I ran it for ten years, but this one unit consumed me, probably to the detriment of my other sites.

Becoming part of the community

In 2014, the Western Tennis Club in Glasgow asked me if I would be interested in opening a coffee bar just beside their grounds in the leafy, prosperous Hyndland area. By this stage my father had passed away and my brother had retired, and now lives in Italy. I sold the Byres Road restaurant and opened the new venture which I named *Café Parma*, and it quickly took on arms and legs, expanding from a coffee shop to a restaurant which I wanted to be a homage to *La Parmigiana* which my brother had sold in 2015. Basically, I wanted it to be a mini *La Parmigiana* but with a less formal, more casual approach. Because we are part of the tennis club, we open at 8am for breakfast as well.

What has evolved, to my delight, is a combination of *La Parmigiana* and *Paperino's*. I still get customers who my dad served as well as customers from the Byres Road venue. Christmas Eve in both venues was always crowded and busy and I now have a mix of customers who book to spend Christmas Eve in Café Parma as early as June. This interview is taking place in early October, and I'm fully booked for Christmas Eve.

I have a great team here at *Café Parma*. My head chef is John Liddel, who's been with me since 1994 and his sous chef, John Bagley, worked for my dad from the age of 15. My General Manager, Rachael Casey has been with me since 2005 when I opened in Byres Road and without her, I couldn't run this place. I've got a good, reliable team which I have a great rapport with. We have a varied drinks bar, and they make brilliant cocktails, which is great because the only cocktail I can make is a Negroni, but these guys can do all the shaking and stirring which I can't do!

My greatest achievement though are my children, Chiara, Luca and Lorenzo and over the years they have all worked at *Cafe Parma* while they were pursuing their studies at university. As at the time of writing my youngest son, Lorenzo, is currently working with me while also studying at university. I very much love working with my children in the restaurant. It confirms to me that the tradition of my family is still strong through the generations – how proud would my grandparents be of what the family have achieved in their name.

The dining scene is moving faster now than ever before. I can't keep up with the number of places that are opening or the new styles that are emerging which is why I'm so lucky to have a sharp, vibrant team that keep me abreast of what's happening elsewhere in the trade.

With the terrace, we're an all-season venue. People can dine al fresco in the summer, while in winter there's a warm cosy ambience with candlelight and the lanterns all lit up exuding a comforting and welcoming atmosphere; it's a lovely site.

For me, though, the most satisfactory element about *Cafe Parma*, in addition to the lovely ambience and the food is that it has become a genuine combination of community café and restaurant, where people can meet and relax. When I had multiple outlets, I felt I couldn't dedicate the time and effort that I'm able to focus on *Cafe Parma*.

Let me give you an example. There's a group of men of a certain age, all retired, and they meet up here every morning without fail and put the world to right. They call themselves "the Parma Hams", and we've become an important if not vital part of those gentlemen's lives. And that goes too for the mothers with their young children coming in for a coffee, a snack and a blether, the young couple on their first date, the family coming in together for a meal, people celebrating a special occasion, and so on.

We're part of the community and recognised as that and that's what I've really wanted to create. If you wanted me to sum it up, I think I've been able to recreate what I aspired to: *La Parmigiana* but in a more, community focused way.

Advice

Be committed and passionate about running a restaurant. Don't do it or regard it as a hobby or just to make money because you won't. You've got to think of your restaurant, café, diner, coffee shop, whatever, as you're second home as you'll spend so many hours there and you've got to enjoy it. You must have a good working environment as you'll spend more time with your staff than your own family and a good atmosphere is essential to entice customers to come back to you. It's a labour of love.

Stefano's favourite dish: A savoury flan from my parent's hometown in northern Italy called *Torta D'erbe*. When

I taste that, I know I'm in Italy. My mother used to cook this finely rolled short crust pastry oven baked with wild bitter spinach and parmigiano Reggiano cheese baked into the crust. Absolutely delicious.

Stefano's favourite drink: Red wine or a Negroni cocktail.

26. MARIO GIZZI: DI MAGGIO'S AND THE REST, AN INDEPENDENT GIANT

From Di Maggio's Restaurants and Amarone to Anchor Line, Topolabamba, Café Andaluz and Barolo, chances are that if you eat out regularly in Glasgow, you will have dined in a restaurant owned by Mario Gizzi. Mario reveals the story behind the growth of one of the largest independent restaurant groups in Scotland.

Beginnings

My great grandparents had seven children. Their oldest son emigrated to Glasgow in the early 1930's and blazed a trail for the Gizzi family. Thereafter, one-by-one, all his brothers, followed him to Scotland. Three of them settled in Glasgow, one moved to Brighton, the other three returned home as they didn't like the weather!

My father, Mario Snr was born in 1937. By that time my grandparents had opened an ice cream factory in Glasgow called *Alpac Cream Ices*, not far from where the Glasgow Royal Infirmary is located. They also owned *Gizzi's Café* which was located in the then famous Parliamentary Road. Today, apart from the hospital, that entire area has been demolished and rebuilt leaving not a trace of either the ice cream factory or the café. My Grandparents also owned a second *Gizzi's Café* in Garscube Road, Maryhill and a third in Rothesay on the Isle of Bute in the Firth of Clyde.

My dad along with his brother Emilio took over the business after my grandfather died suddenly in 1960. They ran the business for a few years but recognised the ice cream industry was changing and big players like Walls and Lyons Maid were beginning to dominate and crowd out the smaller businesses. They decided to sell the business and went their sperate ways.

I was born in 1959 and attended St Aloysius College in Glasgow. When I was at the St Aloysuis Primary School neither my schoolmates nor I liked the school lunches. My mum made the best pastina in brodo which is Italian chicken soup with pasta. I would attend school every day with a flask of this delicious home-made soup. My friends would smell the aroma and before long were asking me if they could have a taste of the soup. They were soon addicted and very quickly, encouraged by my mum, I was bringing in several flasks of this delicious broth every day and selling it by the cup full.

That was my first taste of being an entrepreneur!

Most Italian boys, when they reached the age of 16, left school to join the family business, usually a fish and chip shop or a café or something similar. I decided that wasn't the route for me, much to my father's displeasure, and I decided to stay on at school to sit my O' Grades and Highers enabling me to go on to university to study accountancy.

When I graduated from University, I wanted to become a Chartered Accountant (CA), and I joined an established Scottish accountancy firm called Stevenson & Kyles. I served my apprenticeship with them and sat my professional exams there.

By this stage my dad owned *McNees Bar* in Glasgow's Southside and I would often lend a hand there. I worked in my dad's pub at the weekend while doing my CA training during the week. Working alongside my mum, dad and sister was great experience as it taught me there is no substitute for hard work.

When I qualified as a CA, the senior partner encouraged me to widen my experience and get a job with a larger CA practice and I was fortunate enough to get a job with Price Waterhouse (PW) in Glasgow. They were one of the big six accountancy firms at the time and remain so today despite my involvement.

The night before I was due to start working in PW my mum and dad had a family dinner to celebrate my qualification as an accountant. My uncle Emilio who by now was an established restaurateur in the city (he owned the popular *Gizzi's Grill* in the city as well as the *737 Chip Shop* next door) proposed the toast. After the dinner he had a chat with me which probably changed the course of my life.

He asked me who was I going to work for next. I told him PW. 'Who are they?' he asked. I told him it was Price Waterhouse. 'And whose books do they do?' he inquired. I told him IBM, Caterpillar, and other big multinationals. Then he asked the clincher. 'What will you be earning?' As proud as a peacock, I stuck my chest out and said: '£7,750 per year.' There was a short silence before my uncle came back with: 'I take more than that from the Space Invaders machine in my chippie.'

I went to bed that night with those words from my uncle resonating. Yes, I might be going to work for Price Waterhouse, but I knew it wouldn't be forever.

The rise of *Di Maggio's*

Sure enough, nine months later I left Price Waterhouse and joined forces with dad and my uncle Joe Conetta. To begin with I managed the *Farmhouse* restaurant which was a popular venue in Glasgow city centre. Shortly after that, we got the chance to buy the *Castle Gardens* Chinese restaurant located on Shawlands Cross. I was keen to open a smart casual Italian pizza and pasta themed restaurant which Glasgow had not seen before. My dad decided to step back so I bought him out and Joe and I started Di Maggio's.

We were initially going to name the restaurant, Di Giacomo's after my mother's maiden name, plus it sounded very Italian American which is always popular. But not long before opening the restaurant, Lee (Joe's wife) in her usual, exuberant style, breezed in one day and announced:

'I've got the name!'

What was that we asked her, and she replied: '*Di Maggio's*'. She explained her thinking. It was the name of the internationally famous baseball player Joe Di Maggio, there was his association with Marilyn Monroe his former wife, and to cap it all off, the first syllable of 'Maggio' was "Ma" for Mario followed by "gio" for Joe. It was a stroke of genius and the name was born.

We opened our first *Di Maggio's* in March 1985 in the West End of Glasgow on Ruthven Lane, just off Byres Road. Our plan had been to open the Shawlands restaurant first however, it took us longer than expected to get planning permission and during the delay the site in the West End became available and so we were able to open there first. Di Maggio's in Shawlands opened a couple of months later in May 1985.

We had no idea of what we'd done. Both restaurants became legendary in Glasgow. On a Monday night alone, we could serve 200 to 300 people at each of the two venues. We had a fantastic chef in Pino Livia who helped lay the foundation of the *Di Maggio's* standards. More than that, I had a great relationship with my Uncle Joe. We were Yin and Yang, oil and vinegar, whatever, we just gelled. We both had the same work ethic; we yearned to be successful, and we put in a huge amount of work in those early days.

In hindsight, opening the West End site first was a good decision. It was located at the rear of Ruthven Lane and trade built up slowly allowing us the time to focus on the set up, work out the operational plan and be prepared for when the explosion hit us as both restaurants soon became phenomenally busy.

The business continued to expand. We opened a *Di Maggio's* in Hamilton, outside Glasgow in 1989. But the gamechanger for the business was when we opened our flagship *Di Maggio's* restaurant in Glasgow city centre, at Royal Exchange Square. At that time there weren't many pizzerias in the city centre and the business went from strength to strength.

Beyond *Di Maggio's*. Tapas and the rest

In the late 1990s Joe decided to retire and his son Tony, my first cousin, joined the business. As with my uncle before him, we hit it off and I've now had an incredibly successful partnership with the Conetta family for the last forty years. There are not many business partnerships which last that long.

Tony was a younger man with a more expansive vision. Just after Joe retired, we bought a second site in the West End in Cresswell Lane not far from the *Di Maggio's* in Ruthven Lane. Around the same time, we travelled to visit Joe who was enjoying his retirement in Spain. We enjoyed the whole Tapas dining scene in Malaga. At that time a new tapas chain called *La Tasca* had recently opened in the city centre and had become extremely popular. Tony came up with the idea of turning the newly acquired West End site into a tapas restaurant.

I was doubtful at first. I pointed out: 'It's tapas. What do we know about Spanish food?' Tony's response was simple: 'A prawn's a prawn. It's just cooked in a different way.' That clinched it and we decided to embark on a new tapas concept.

We named the new West End site *Café Andaluz* which was our first step to diversifying into other cuisines and styles. A second opened just off George Square in Glasgow city centre where the famous *Vesuvio Ristorante* had been located. It gave us the inspiration to open a third *Café Andaluz* on George Street in Edinburgh. Traditionally, Edinburgh restaurateurs only traded in Edinburgh and Glasgow restaurateurs stuck to Glasgow. We were one of the first hospitality businesses to trade in both. Effectively, we chanced our luck by doing this, but, thankfully, it worked and continued the success.

We had already opened a sister Italian brand, *Amarone*, in Glasgow and on the back of our success in Edinburgh, we opened a second *Amarone* restaurant on St Andrews square in Edinburgh. Since then, we've opened another two *Café Andaluz* in Edinburgh and one each in Aberdeen and Newcastle. The fruits of all that were borne from the hard work that the family put in during those early years.

We then acquired the ground and basement of the Anchor Line Building in Glasgow. It had lain lay dormant for several years due to issues with the building itself. Tony had the idea of refurbishing the space which had been the former luxurious first-class booking offices of the transatlantic shipping company called *Anchor Line* and transforming it into a bar and restaurant named after the shipping line. This and the *Atlantic Brasserie* below, as well as the *Citizen* next door have become very much part of the Glasgow dining scene.

Along the way, Tony and I went into partnership in a second restaurant group (Hunky Dory Dining) with another cousin Paul Sloan and his friend Calum MacLachlainn. Together we opened the Tex-Mex restaurant called *Topolabamba* in St Vincent Street. That gave us the confidence and inspiration to open more restaurants on that same block.

Since then, we have opened an Indian restaurant, we describe as a "Bombay Café" called *Chaakoo* and the other is a Thai small plates venue called *Panang*. All three are very popular, particularly with the Instagram generation.

Remembering what Tony said about cooking a prawn in different ways? Well, we have certainly managed to take that idea to new heights. I'm delighted to say all three sites are doing very well.

Across the two groups we employ about eleven hundred people, with 30 outlets and two hotels. We are very lucky to have some great people working in the venues and at exec team level which gives the business a solid base and enables us to expand.

The most important partnership I have is with my wife, Vivion. She allows me the freedom to develop my hobby which is my work.

My Denzil Washington Moment

One Friday afternoon in February 2012, shortly before Valentine's Day, I received a phone call from one of my area managers telling me I had to get up to *Amarone* immediately. I asked him 'why?' He replied there was a customer in there with a bomb!

I ran up there and all the staff were waiting outside, the chefs in their whites, alarms ringing. I met the area manager, and we walked round the side of the restaurant where we could see through some windows. Sure enough the chap was sitting there on his own at a high table. I asked the area manager for an update, and he told me the police were on their way.

This was a nightmare; a Friday three days before Valentine's Day! I said to my managers and senior staff 'I'm going in.' This is what I call my Denzil Washington moment.

I went in and down the stairs to a half-landing, the fire alarms going crazy and saw the guy with his head down at the table. I shouted and asked him what he was doing.

He shuffled sideways and pointed to his coat, saying he had a 'bomb' in there. I questioned this and he replied.

'Come down here and I'll show you.'

My response was: 'No, I'm going to stay here on the half-landing, but I don't believe you've got a bomb. The police are on their way. If you don't leave now, you're going to end up in serious trouble. I'm happy if you walk away, leave this restaurant and I never see you again. I won't recognise you.'

He looked at me and said:

'No, I'm staying.'

I walked back outside just as the police were arriving with their protective shields. They took me to a mobile police command van and asked me the layout of the building, how you switch the power on and off and a dozen other questions. Once I'd answered them all, they said I would need to stay in the van.

I asked them what was happening, and they said they couldn't force the issue. If they did that, he might detonate the bomb which would close down the city and have huge repercussions. Instead, they would have to wait it out. With luck, they said, he might drink enough of the red wine in the restaurant to fall asleep.

At this point, my wife phoned asking where I was. I'd promised her faithfully I would be home in time for tea that night. So, I had to explain that I might be a bit late. She asked me 'what was my excuse now?" I replied:

'There's a guy with a bomb in…' And that's as far as I got before she slammed the phone down on me!

Later, I was taken to police headquarters and placed in an incident room. About a couple of hours later, by which time it was about nine o' clock, my phone went again, and it was my wife. She said frantically:

'Mario, Mario, there's a guy with a bomb in an Italian restaurant in the city centre!' I said to her, 'I've been trying to tell you that!'

That was my siege negotiator Denzil Washington moment, and it didn't work. The guy eventually gave himself up and thankfully the incident ended peacefully.

Reflection

We've had great success in Glasgow and expanding to four cities across the UK. Our success has been the result of hard work and having a great team around you. But it's also stemmed from a family with dedication and commitment over the years. It may be myself who is being interviewed for this book, but equally the credit should also go to my partners, namely my cousin Tony, my Uncle Joe before him, his wife Lee and not least my own mother and father. Our success is a product of all their endeavours and determination to succeed through the decades.

Advice

You must have the hunger to come into this business. It is a lot more challenging, competitive and an expensive industry to enter than it was 40 or 50 years ago. People are far more familiar with Italian food today than they were back then. I recall customers asking for Spaghetti Bolognese and insisting they did not want it with garlic as an additive. Taste buds have certainly changed.

Finance is not the most romantic or attractive aspect of the hospitality business, but it is essential you keep on top of the pennies. The three key ingredients here are turnover, gross profit and labour. You need to be on top of all three on at least a weekly basis to know your weekly turnover and staff costs in order to make a profit or even survive. More recently utilities, rates and other business costs have increased so much over the years monthly accounts are vital to keep the business on track.

You also need a good team around you to look after the finances and operations but above all you need to get across to the public, your customer, the one vital message which is the flavour of your food and the style of your service. Get those right and you're on your way.

Mario's favourite dish: Spaghetti with lobster.

Mario's favourite wine: French Burgandy or Spanish Rioja.

27. BRIAN MAULE: FINE DINING AT ITS BEST

Highly regarded and respected in the industry, Brian worked with the legendary Roux Brothers, Albert & Michel, before taking on Chef de Cuisine with Michel Roux Jr in London for 15 years. Then it was time to move back to Glasgow and run his own renowned fine dining restaurant, Chandon d'or for 22 years. In his own words he talks openly about his journey and the challenges along the way.

Beginnings

I was born in Stevenson, in Ayrshire on the west coast of Scotland. I enjoyed school, but for all the wrong reasons, such as the social side. I left school having just sat my 'O' Grades but was fortunate to get a Youth Training Scheme (YTS) apprenticeship at The *Skean Dhu* in Irvine, Ayrshire.

My food knowledge prior to starting the YTS was very limited, it was more a eat to live, rather than live to eat philosophy. I couldn't really say I wanted to work in cuisine. It was just something I fell into with the YTS scheme, and I ended up working in a kitchen. But I found myself enjoying it and I got promoted quite quickly and was eager to learn more.

Three of us on the YTS scheme became close friends and after a while, we came up with the bright idea of going to Switzerland and working in the kitchens there. However, at that time you needed a visa to work, but to get a visa you had to have a job over there. But to get a job, you needed a, guess what? A visa! It was a classic Catch 22 situation.

Instead, we pooled together a thousand pounds and went to France, Lyon to be precise, the culinary capital of the world, without a job, a place to stay, or a word of French. We ended up in a youth hostel in Lyon, which allowed us to get our heads down for the first couple of days. Then we just knocked on the doors of restaurants, bars and hotels looking for kitchen work. A chap at one of the places we tried offered one of us a job if the other two also found work. He gave us the numbers and names of chefs in Lyons. All of us were successful and we got jobs in the top three restaurants in Lyons., all of which had either a two or three Michelin Star rating. We found accommodation; a cramped studio flat where I had to share a bed for a year. Nice and cosy it sure wasn't but we weren't in that bed long each night after the 18-hour days!

I picked up French working in the kitchen, but it was difficult as only one guy there had a smattering of English. At that time in Lyons, 30 years ago, very few people spoke English. Aside from trying to pick up the language, it was daunting, and the hours were long, from 7 in the morning to 1 the following morning six days a week. I was so tired I didn't appreciate what I was learning, but I was determined, my learning curve was steep, and I was keen to live the French way. Working in a kitchen at a high-class restaurant in Lyon was probably the best foundation for doing that. My bosses could see I was open minded and willing to learn all the techniques required and I acquired a respect for the produce and the many ways it can be cooked and served, which is vital to pick up in that environment if you are going to get on.

Working with the Roux Brothers

Lyon lasted 18 months and after that I went to work for the Roux Brothers in London at *Le Gavroche* which was the first three-starred Michelin restaurant in Britain. I managed to get that position through my boss in Lyon, as I'd translated an article from an English magazine on French chefs for him. At the time he was the President of the Master Chefs of France. In return he offered to help me find a job when an opportunity arose in London. He kept to his word and arranged for the interview with the Roux Brothers. I was successful and stayed with the brothers for the next 15 years.

I started quite raw with the brothers as my French was still basic and most of the waiters and chefs were French and all the orders were called out in French, but my experience with the cooking did me no harm. London is a hard slog. It's fast and you must want to learn. Fortunately, I did and with the brothers I got promoted quite fast from first commis chef to *chef de partie*.

Michael Roux sent me to learn at restaurants in France and Belgium which was a great experience and when the head chef at *Le Gavroche* retired I stepped into his position. I was head chef there for a total of eight years, but there were many tears along the way.

Faux Pas at *Le Gavroche*

I remember one Christmas when I was still *chef de partie*, there was the usual private parties at the two upstairs rooms at *Le Gavroche* which could hold up to 25 people. We were in the middle of serving one of those rooms by making a vegetable mousse with langoustine prawns and potato coley, all to be served on a large silver plate. I finished it off with salad and herbs and told the girl I was working with to serve it to the guests in the private room. Two minutes later the head chef came back and nearly threw the trolley at me with some choice language. The girl had placed the silver plate with the vegetable mousse on a hot plate!

Fortunately, I had exactly that amount of produce left in the fridge to re-dress and serve another mousse, but it meant there was none for the a la carte service at the restaurant – serious stress! You guessed it, just as I had finished remaking the mousse, with tears in my eyes, somebody ordered mousse for dinner. Any remaining stock we had to make that dish again was in the freezer. I had to test it first to see if I could serve it - luckily, I could. So, I had to make yet another vegetable mousse and sent it out as fast as I could. It was the worst service I ever had, and I still had tears in my eyes an hour-and-a-half later. The stress that day was through the roof.

You learn a lot from disasters like that, not least who to trust but also how to organise yourself better. That whole incident occurred purely because of a stupid mistake over a hotplate. You can't trust people too much and you need to always ensure you're in control of the entire section. Sure, I felt like walking out at the time, but I learned a lot from it.

At *Le Gavroche* we had a lot of politicians as guests including prime ministers of the day. We also had members of the Royal Family, including Princess Diana and the Queen Mother. It's too easy for a lot of chefs and owners to get carried away with celebrity. For me everyone who crosses the door in your restaurant are as important as they're paying guests. My wife could never understand why I never got excited when a celebrity was in. But to me all the customers are the same.

Glasgow

After 15 years in London with the Roux Brothers, I wanted to open my own restaurant in Glasgow, *Chandon d'or* and harness all the experience and knowledge I'd acquired to make it one of the best places in town, which I think I achieved, but only after a lot of hard work.

I opened in Glasgow in 2001, three weeks before 9/11; not the best time to open a restaurant. Then, a few years later, there were the bank crashes. But we got through it. Things change rapidly. To take one example, there's a lot more dietary requirements or food fashions people have now than before, veganism being a classic example. Or people not wanting garlic. You must adapt to such changes; see them as a positive challenge, not a barrier.

In my Glasgow venue I had up to twelve chefs to cover the upstairs and downstairs sections (where the private rooms were and where we could host up to three parties)

I placed a great emphasis on service. I would say to front of house staff, we make your job easy by cooking excellent food which the customers love. The result is very few complaints for you to deal with at the tables. I encouraged them to use that time to engage with the customers, because service is the next most important thing in this trade after the quality of the food. Too many times in the past few years in bars and other restaurants, I've seen managers getting dragged from table to table because of complaints. I was desperate to avoid that and make the welcome at *Chandon d'or* the best in Glasgow and I think I succeeded.

To make that work it's imperative that the kitchen and front of house are working together as one, singing from the same hymn sheet. It's a team effort not the kitchen against the dining room or vice versa. At *Chandon D'or* I made it very clear, there was only one person dictating, and that was me.

Working with and mentoring young people

I do believe that young people working in kitchens were willing to learn more in previous years than they are now. I think there's an element today of young people walking away because it's either too hard or too strict. As I say to my own children, the only way to succeed is to learn by your mistakes and in our industry that's the only way to learn. I think a lot of people, especially young people put life before work. That's fine up to a point, but that won't get you nice holidays or clothes or a good car, the things that people aspire to. Only dedicated and committed hard work will achieve that.

I'm proud to say that a lot of the young people I've worked with and trained have gone onto good positions, both here and abroad. When I closed my restaurant in Glasgow recently, I received up to forty messages from people I'd worked with in the past who said they wouldn't be where they were now without me, which is really lovely to hear.

At the time they were working with me a lot of them probably thought I was a monster. But, as I said to many of them at the time, they won't appreciate what they've learned until they leave me. Once they've left, they'll realise how quick, efficient, tidy and above all, *organised* they are when they go into another kitchen because of what they've learned under me, which I also had to learn the hard way.

For twelve years I was involved in a Culinary Excellence programme with Glasgow City Council. This involved taking up to twenty young people, aged 15-17, into the kitchen for three months where they learned all about front of house, how to cook, how to serve and create a menu so that by the end of the three months they would be ready to cook and serve a lunch for 20 people at the restaurant for local councillors, businesspeople, and others. I would arrange for the media to be present covering the occasion.

These kids came from deprived areas of the city and when they first came in, I'd ask them as a group what they wanted from this experience, and I couldn't get a word out of any of them. After the three months the transformation in their self-esteem and self-confidence was incredible. Before the actual big lunch, the staff and I would get half of them to do a dummy run at the front of house and half in the kitchen one week and then alternate them the next week, so they all got experience of both.

For the big day I would choose who would be serving and who would be in the kitchen. After the lunch was over, we would have a dinner for them as a thank you. Seeing the change in them was magnificent and even if they didn't come into the industry, I believe it gave them a tremendous boost for their future.

Regrettably, the Council stopped the programme and when the restaurant closed some of the kids also emailed me with their regrets about that but also thanked me for the opportunity they'd be given. I was very moved by that.

Unfortunately, the restaurant closed in 2023 and the response to that was an eye- opener to me not just, as I've said from customers but also from social media like Linked In and other outlets. There was a whole series of factors behind the closure but the significant drop-off in the lunch trade caused by covid and working from home was a major reason. Another factor was the falloff in businesses using the private rooms downstairs for meetings and presentations which just collapsed with lockdown and never recovered.

But I thoroughly enjoyed the 22 years *Chandon D'or* was open. It was a tremendous and unforgettable experience and I was extremely proud to be serving up the best fine dining experience to the people of Glasgow and all those who came into the city.

Advice
Be committed, be determined, don't be afraid to make mistakes. Above all, you must want to learn and show that willingness to learn.

Brian's favourite dish: Believe it or not Cheesy Beano toast - No kidding!

Brian's favourite wine: Any red wine from the Cote du Rhone area of France.

Printed in Great Britain
by Amazon